SO-FQN-861

A
PATCHWORK
QUILT

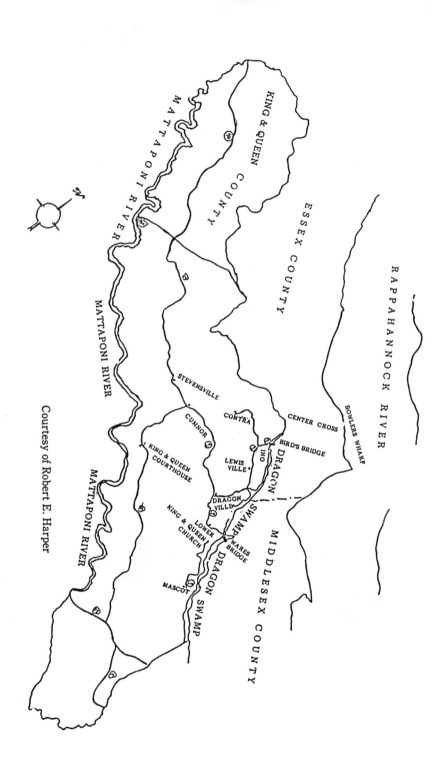

MATTAPONI RIVER

MATTAPONI RIVER

MATTAPONI RIVER

KING & QUEEN COUNTY

ESSEX COUNTY

RAPPAHANNOCK RIVER

STEVENSVILLE

CUMNOR

CONTRA

CENTER CROSS

BOWLERS WHARF

BIRD'S BRIDGE

KING & QUEEN COURTHOUSE

LEWIS VILLE

INO

DRAGON SWAMP

DRAGON VILLE

MIDDLESEX COUNTY

KING & QUEEN CHURCH

LOWER

WARES BRIDGE

DRAGON SWAMP

MASCOT

Courtesy of Robert E. Harper

Lousie E. Gray

A PATCHWORK QUILT

Life on a Virginia Farm
1910-1920

Louise Eubank Gray

𝔅𝔯𝔲𝔫𝔰𝔴𝔦𝔠𝔨

Copyright © 1989 by Louise Eubank Gray

All rights reserved. No part of this book may be reproduced in any form or by any means, electronic or mechanical, including photocopying or by any informational storage or retrieval system, without written permission from the author and the publisher.

International Standard Book Number
1-55618-061-6

Library of Congress Catalog Card Number
89-61308

First Printing, August 1989
Second Printing, October 1989

First Original Edition

Published in the United States of America

by

Brunswick Publishing Corporation
RT. 1, BOX 1A1
LAWRENCEVILLE, VIRGINIA 23868

To

Doug and Vel, Trippy and John

Lewisville, circa 1960
(Birthplace of the author; it burned in 1967)

DEAR HOUSE

Dark hands hewed sills and rafters;
Strong hands sawed cypress for its frame;
Skilled hands formed bricks for chimneys tall,
Split shingles from white oak hearts.
The woods rang with sounds of men at work,
And from their labors rose a house
To shelter many beneath its kindly roof.

My grandparents reared their children here
Beside its blazing hearth's bright warmth.
They opened wide its friendly doors
To welcome passersby, their neighbors, or their kin.
The stately carriage, cart, or creaking wagon
Drew rein before its door with equal grace;
For no one failed to find a welcome at this house.
Children romped happily through its halls.
The aged dozed securely on its porch.
The drift of wood smoke from its chimney
Scented the morning air;
This house saw decades mark a century or more.

Now fire has brought it down,
Reduced to ash the cypress and the oak.
Its hospitable doors will welcome none again,
But memory can rebuild it in a flash,
More bright without a trace of time's decay.
And so it stands with all its homely marks;
Flooded in the gold of love,
And so it shall remain
Untouched by change.

Acknowledgments

The material in *A Patchwork Quilt* is based on personal recollections; however, from the dwindling number of my contemporaries I have supplemented my memory about certain details. I thank John Pollard Garrett, in particular, for information on the cultivation of corn and the process of cleaning the well; and Ruth B. St. John for details about housekeeping. I have also referred to several publications about game conditions in the first quarter of the twentieth century, making molasses, the Dragon, and World War I to avoid factual errors.

Special recognition is due Robert R. Harper for his beautifully drawn map of my part of King and Queen County and to Helen White, who typed the manuscript, much of it from handwritten copy, and who willingly made corrections and changes. I am especially grateful to Bettie Woodward James, whose century-old patchwork quilt is pictured on the cover, and to Larry Chowning, Margaret T. Rudd, and Ellen Anderson whose interest, encouragement and assistance have been invaluable.

In addition I wish to express appreciation to many friends who offered encouragement and assistance: to Jane Flower Deringer, faculty member of Rappahannock Community College, to Olivia Jarvis for hours of proofreading, to Barbara LeCompte Nelson for typing parts of the manuscript, and to Margaret M. Benson, who secured pamphlets and information when I needed it.

I recognize too the patience of my publishers, Dr. Walter J. Raymond and his wife, Marianne S. Raymond, who bore with me and my demands with cooperation and good humor.

The acknowledgments would not be complete, however, without an expression of my in debtedness to my parents, relatives, neighbors, and even the farm workers, all long gone, but who formed the fabric, the warp and woof, of my early years. In their daily living, they demonstrated principles of industry, thrift, dependability and common sense, but deeper and more important, were the values they lived by: integrity, morality, kindness, and concern for others.

This was the era when a man's word was his bond, and a good reputation was more valuable than money. These people did not attain wealth, power, or fame, but they left good names and standards to live by which have enriched my life and the lives of their descendants.

Finally, to my family I wish to express gratitude for their understanding and sympathy. It is really for them that the project was initiated. If the account seems to be slightly rose-tinted, it is due to the characteristic of memory to block out the dark times and to burnish the bright ones.

Contents

Foreword

There is a certain mystique about a patchwork quilt. In many families it is a priceless heirloom, treasured for its beauty, associations, and workmanship.

My quilt is a fabric of a different sort, a rich pattern of scenes, people, activities, experiences, and dreams. It becomes visible through the power of memory and of words and becomes an heirloom only through the cognizance of my descendants as they contrast their way of life with mine.

The twentieth century came late to many parts of Virginia. In isolated pockets life went on for two or three decades much as it had before the turn of the century. Aristocratic families as well as poorer ones read by oil lamps and traveled by horse and buggy while not many miles away other families enjoyed electricity and indoor plumbing. Life style was due as much to geography as to affluence.

A Patchwork Quilt describes the day-by-day life of a single family in a community typical of the region during the decade, 1910-1920. The focus is not on events but on customs, conventions, attitudes, and practices in this little known period.

Public attention, directed to great social changes brought on by World War I, the Depression, and World War II, all before the half-century mark, has overlooked a period of time in Virginia when life was quiet but colorful, uneventful but real, vigorous but happy.

In this country life has changed more drastically in the last three quarters of a century than in the previous three hundred years. The world has been brought closer together, but the family unit has been torn asunder. Family ties once formed a close knit web weakened by death but strengthened by each marriage and birth. Children were taught to know their relatives, to claim kin to third and fourth cousins. Relatives kept in touch by letter even though many miles separated them. Visiting was frequent if distance permitted. The saying "blood is thicker than water," was literally true. Today family relationships are much less important.

Farm life establishes the work ethic. The livestock, the crops, even the land itself, depend upon the care of the farmer. When droughts come, crops fail, disease strikes, the farm family has to cope, struggling through the bad times in expectation of better. There is no such thing as giving up. Shirking responsibility is a cardinal sin; integrity and reliability are survival traits.

Into such a world I was born and lived until adulthood. Its conventions and values shaped my life; its traditions and attitudes still retain a hold upon me.

Louise Eubank Gray

April 27, 1989

CHAPTER I

Summertime

I noticed the smell of the locust blossoms as soon as I got out of bed. Running to the window, I looked out; the old trees stood higher than the house with clusters of blossoms hanging like bunches of grapes from the gnarled limbs almost touching the window.

"It's summer! It's summer," I sang because to me summer started when the locusts were in bloom and I could go barefoot.

"If it's warm tomorrow, you can take off your shoes," my mother had said, adding "during the middle of the day."

I hurried to dress; I was not allowed downstairs until I was fully clothed, and this was not accomplished in a minute. I dropped my flannel nightgown, threw the horrid assafetida bag behind the bureau, and pulled on the hated long underwear, its long sleeves bagging at the wrists and drawers stretched around the ankles. Black stockings had to go over the underwear, and it took time to lap the loose ribbing at the ankles and pull up the heavy stockings over my knees. The stockings were kept up with garters, a length of black elastic measured to fit my legs and sewed together by Aunt Gay, my mother's sister. Next came the high buttoned shoes. In my hurry I fumbled with the button hook and finally left several unbuttoned spots. Today, maybe, I could take them off for the summer. A white petticoat with a ruffled flounce was next and finally my dress, and I was almost ready.

The washstand held a pitcher half-full of cold water, and I quickly washed my face and brushed my teeth. The waste water went into a big china slopjar. Later I would have to take this out, empty it, wash the jar, and leave it to air in the violet bed in the garden, along with the chamber pots from the other bedrooms.

Having run a comb through my hair, I clattered down stairs where Mother was putting breakfast on the table. A large pan of batter bread was on a plate to be taken to the dining room, biscuits were browning in the oven, a dozen sausage cakes were on a platter, and coffee was bubbling in the blue enameled pot on the Majestic range. Mother was setting the place at the kitchen table for Connie, the hired man; and Aunt Gay was skimming cream from a gallon brown crock. She held the skimmer carefully as she poured the cream into a large pitcher.

"As soon as John comes with the milk, we'll eat," said Mother.

At that moment my father entered with a ten-quart bucket of fresh milk in each hand. Mother set out several large bowls and strained the milk into them. Then after my father had washed, we went to the table.

My father said grace. Never in all my years of growing up was I asked to say grace, (none of the women were), but it was an unfailing part of the meal-time ritual. My father never hurried; we sat with bowed heads until Amen was pronounced, and he began to serve the food.

"Mother, may I go barefoot today? Can I take off the underwear? Please. It's going to be warm. Please." The thought of wearing that underwear and those shoes another day was unbearable.

Auntie looked sympathetic. My mother said, "We'll see."

As the day advanced, it grew warmer. At eleven o'clock I approached Mother again.

"Please, Mother. It's so hot I'm melting. Please let me take off the underwear and go barefoot."

At her nod, I scampered upstairs and quickly unbottoned my dress. Off came the hated shoes, the black stockings, the dress, the horrid underwear. I dressed again and ran out into the sunshine feeling like a butterfly that had escaped its chrysalis at last.

For the moment, it was heaven to feel free, unencumberd. Pounds lighter, it seemed. I skipped about on the grass inhaling the perfume of the locust blossoms and rejoicing in summer's arrival.

I had been named Louise Virginia Eubank, but half the time my parents called me Baby, a pet name that they used until long after I was grown. My first name was for my mother's spinster sister, Louise Gay Walden, whom all the nieces and nephews called Auntie. Sixteen years older than Mother, she lived with us or, more properly, we lived with her because the house had been her inheritance when their mother died. Aunt Gay was my champion and defender throughout my childhood. My mother, who did not want to rear a spoiled child, so she said, became a rather severe disciplinarian. Whippings were frequent, and I remember Auntie shielding my legs with her hands and catching the licks meant for me. Her protests did not deter my mother who let the blows fall where they would. According to mother, I was both stubborn and hard-headed and required vigorous correction. I was sent so often to fetch a switch that the spirea bush (from which I usually chose it, because the twigs were brittle and broke easily,) became a scraggly, forlorn, and decimated shrub.

I was not pretty either. My skin was pale, my straight blond hair was fine and hard to manage, and my eyes were blue. My mother had hoped that my eyes would be brown like my father's. She strove mightily to overcome the handicap of my looks. "You're ugly, but you must try to be good," she would say. "Pretty is as pretty does" was quoted to me at least twice a day. At times I wondered if I would not be a failure in both categories.

My mother was a strong-minded, determined woman, but she was gentle and loving, too. I think she had to discipline herself in order to live up to her image of a responsible parent. She lived in a state of constant apprehension that I would perform some foolhardy and fatal act. "Louise is so venturesome," she would say with some justice because I loved to climb trees, ride horses, explore the swamp, hang on the back of the wagon, tease the dogs, or find some other excitement. "The Lord looks after children and fools," Mother would say, "and that is the only thing that's saved Louise."

Going barefoot was a joy after the first few days when tender feet had become accustomed to rough paths and coarse grass. I skipped happily to the barn, the wood pile, and to the hen house. Best of all was to run across the field to Marguerite's house.

Our nearest neighbors were my uncle's family on the adjoining farm. Uncle Richie was my mother's brother, and he and his wife Aunt Hettie had three children: Martha, the oldest, named for our mutual grandmother; then there was Dick; and last, Marguerite, two years older than I, but my playmate and a strong influence in my life. "If Marguerite told Louise to stick her head in the fire, she would certainly do it," my mother often said whenever Marguerite had led me into some mischief. I was a willing follower, however, in most situations.

Aunt Het, Marguerite's mother, loved all animal life. At her house was sure to be an assortment of baby creatures: fluffy just-hatched chicks, ducks, maybe even guineas; Old Oscar, the gander, and Maude, the mother goose, would have their brood of goslings out nibbling the fresh grass. Marguerite and I would revel in the freedom of the outdoors.

There were hazards, however, to going barefoot. A farm was not always a neat place; pieces of boards were lying about, perhaps broken planks from a chicken coop, a pig pen, or a cow stall with a rusty nail protruding. Bits of glass from long-broken window panes, sharp thorns from locust trees, or splinters often caused minor wounds. Always inclined to rush headlong into what I was doing, I often had a cut foot or worse, a nail puncture.

"Louise, if you cut your foot one more time you'll have to wear your shoes," my mother had said only yesterday. This was a serious threat because my mother was meticulous about living up to her word, and she had not said maybe.

"What is wrong with your foot, Baby?" she asked on Tuesday when she saw me limping a little.

"Nothing," I answered promptly, hoping she would let the matter drop.

"Come here. Let me see." There was a rising note in her voice that boded no good.

"You've stuck a nail in your foot, and you told me that nothing was wrong when I asked you. You've told me a story, and I'll have to whip you for that," she said resignedly. "Go bring me a switch."

I limped off to the spirea bush, as usual. Such errands were common and I did not dread the whipping much because when Mother had lived up to her word and administered the punishment, it was not severe. What bothered me was the threat of shoes!

"Now, let me clean that foot," Mother said, the whipping over.

"Sister, get the carbolic acid and some toothpicks, please," she directed Aunt Gay as she prepared a large basin of hot water.

My foot by that time of day was dark with dirt from running over dew-wet paths where dogs, cats, and chickens had been scurrying about. Sure enough, there was a black spot with an angry red ring around it.

"Louise, when did you stick the nail in your foot?" Alarm was already in her voice. A nail puncture was a potentially serious injury because there were no tetanus shots. A wound, left untended, could result in lockjaw, which usually would be fatal.

"Yesterday," I quavered, sorry now that I had not mentioned it and let her use the iodine that stung so dreadfully.

"Kate, you'll have to open the wound and disinfect it," said Auntie.

"Please, please, don't do that," I begged. From previous experience, I knew what was ahead. Tetanus baccilli develop only when shut away from air; a wound which had closed had to be probed and left open.

"Hold still," said Mother in a strained voice, "I'll try to be quick."

Auntie held my hand while I screamed, but Mother was firm and swift.

It was a week before I could walk on my foot again. The treatment had to be repeated every day so that healing might take place from the bottom of the wound. When I was able to scamper about again, I tried hard to be careful.

My mother dealt successfully with minor wounds, cuts, scratches, stings, and bites in most instances. She doctored colds with castor oil, fevers with quinine, and an upset stomach with calomel. The doctor was not called except for serious conditions. When I fell from the cherry tree and broke my arm, it was serious enough to require a doctor. How well I remember!

Both black heart and red heart cherries were ripe. The trees were loaded with fruit and Mother used a common method of getting fruit picked: "one-half for the other."

This meant that the owner of the trees gave the picker one-half of the fruit for the picking. Aunt Susan and her daughters, Jenny Bell and Viney, were eager to pick and so was I. Climbing trees was one of my chief delights, so why not combine this pleasure with something useful. I had my own bucket, and I had picked several quarts when I suddenly leaned forward to reach a beautiful cluster just out of reach. The branch on which I pressed was rotten, and so I pitched headlong to the ground.

"Lord'a'Mercy! Louise done fell out the tree. Run, Viney. Run for Miss Kate," shrieked Aunt Susan from her perch above me. Viney, according to the story frequently related afterwards, was on the ground emptying her bucket. She set off at a fast lope, her fat hips shaking. Jenny Bell, who was up the red heart cherry tree, scrambled down, eager to be part of the excitement. She and Aunt Susan bent over my lifeless form. Stunned, I lay motionless. When I began to come to, I saw my mother's anguished face as she reached my side. Badly frightened, she was sure that the dire calamity which she had feared for so long was upon her.

"Thank Gawd," breathed Viney as she ran up, "She ain't daid."

"She hurt bad. Better go after Mis' Shubank," Aunt Susan muttered.

"Yes, Viney, you run to the back field and get Mr. Eubank. Tell him to come at once. We will have to send for the doctor," I heard my mother say breathlessly.

"I'll car'y her to de house, Miss Kate," said Jenny Bell as she lifted me in her strong arms and followed my mother; the others fell in behind.

Auntie, who had been reading on the front porch, heard the approaching commotion. "Take care, Jenny Bell, don't mash dat arm," Aunt Susan admonished loudly.

At last we reached the house. At each mention of the doctor, I wailed," I don't want Dr. DeShazo. He'll laugh at me. Please call Dr. Brooksie."

We never had Dr. Brooksie; in fact, there was a coolness between our families. I knew him well because he was Marguerite's uncle by marriage, and I saw him often at her house. He was old and kind, and I wanted him and no one else.

I loved Dr. DeShazo dearly. He had brought me into the world and had ministered to all the family ills for as long as I could remember. However, he loved to tease me, and I knew he would laugh at me for having fallen out of the tree.

"Please get Dr. Brooksie," I begged, and my distraught parents yielded to my pleas without much objection.

My father saddled his horse and went off to find Dr. Brooksie who, Viney said, was "up yonder at Uncle Combs' house." A couple of hours later, the doctor arrived, tied his horse by the front gate, and entered the house.

Dr. Brooksie had a white goatee, a moustache, tired blue eyes, and a gentle smile. He always stuttered a little.

"What's a cherry picker like-like-you doing here in bed?" he asked, but he did not laugh.

He set the bone without an anesthetic, or a shot, to dull the pain. To help matters somewhat, my father, a teetotaler, made a great concession. I could have a little whiskey beforehand. Auntie produced a bottle from some hiding place and mixed a toddy with sugar and water for me. I thought it was very good. It did little to lessen the pain when the bone snapped into place, but it did help me to go to sleep afterwards.

My arm was in splints, not a cast, for several weeks, and Dr. Brooksie stopped by daily as he passed through our farm making calls on his patients five or six miles away. He would sit on the front porch, remove the splint, let my arm rest on the arm of the old rocker, and bathe it in alcohol; then he wrapped it tightly again.

"Dr. Brooksie, would you like a glass of buttermilk?" I would ask. "I think Mother has just finished churning."

"Thank you, yes. Some buttermilk would be fine." I'd hurry to bring him a glass of cool buttermilk with little golden flecks of butter floating in it. Usually there would be a piece of cake or a ham biscuit to go with it. He seemed to enjoy the visit and the refreshments. It was all the pay he took. After a rest on the porch, he would be on his way again. My arm healed straight and strong, thanks to him, but he was never called in again. Dr. DeShazo remained our doctor.

I spent most summer days with Marguerite. Our favorite haunt was a little stream that originated in a spring near her house. A huge sycamore tree stood at the head of the spring; its roots held the soil together over a horse-shoe shaped bank which surrounded the bowl of the spring. There the shade was cool and deep. Little ferns and mosses grew up the bank and a tiny, steady stream of water dripped into the pool. Aunt Het often set her churn here to cool, coming later to sit under the sycamore's shade and rhythmically work the dasher until the butter came, while Marguerite and I played in the water downstream.

As we grew older, we ventured farther away. Sometimes we dammed the water with a few pieces of fallen tree branches, earth, bits of broken bricks, or whatever we could find, and felt excitement and accomplishment when the water became a few inches deep. The dam soon washed away, but we had felt like engineers while we constructed it. Of course, the fun was in the doing, and we could build another dam tomorrow.

Small green frogs, which lived along the banks of the stream, were my special interest. We spent hours splashing about in the stream catching them and taking them home. I got into difficulty with my father more than once because I had put frogs in the horse trough.

My summer days, however, were not all play. I was called on constantly to run errands. "Go to the barn and tell Connie to hitch Mac to the buggy." "Bring a fresh bucket of water from the well." "Sweep the door yard." "Take these apple peelings to the hogs." "Call the company to dinner." "Run to the garden and bring me three onions." My fat legs were kept running from pillar to post meeting the demands of the adult members of the household. However, I also had some specific chores for which I was held responsible, although they were done under strict supervision.

Late in the afternoon I gathered eggs. We kept a flock of 25 or 30 laying hens most of the time. When a hen became two or three years old and stopped laying, she was culled from the flock and, along with others, would be shipped by boat to Baltimore to be sold. The size of the flock varied from time to time, but in summer the hens were usually laying well. The hen house where the hens roosted at night had a row of nest boxes where they were supposed to lay; but many, like people, chose to depart from the norm. Several nested in the hay barn choosing a spot as well-hidden and difficult to reach as possible. Others showed even greater originality. One old "Dominecker" regularly laid her egg on the seat of the riding-plow when it was not in use. An old folded bag formed a sort of cushion for the seat, and thus made it seem a suitable nest to the hen, although the egg often rolled off and broke. When I heard a cackle from the shed where the plow stood, I made a mad dash to retrieve the egg if possible.

A hen always cackled when she had laid an egg. This made locating the nest a little easier. "I heard a hen cackling in the orchard a while ago," Auntie might say. "Better see if you can find the nest before something gets the egg." Off I would go, parting thick weeds, lifting heavy branches of blackberry vines, and peering into fence corners. At last, I would return with the egg, having learned where to look the next day.

Egg-gathering was a kind of treasure hunt, and finding a new nest with several eggs in it was an exciting event, worthy to be recounted at the supper table.

Another of my duties was to shut up the chicken coops at night. We usually had several flocks of chickens of varying ages housed in coops around the barnyard. When a hen hatched her chicks, she was provided a coop for her brood until they were feathered out and ready to go their own way. Predators, such as rats, foxes, and weasels would sometimes destroy eight or ten chickens at a time if they could get to them. I had to see that each coop was closed and blocked with a brick at night; next morning after the dew had dried, the coops were unfastened and the hens and chickens fed and watered.

Chickens that ranged the yard before the dew had dried tended to get "the gaps," as we called it. They would stand gasping for breath instead of busily looking for food as healthy birds did. When Mother spotted a chicken with "gaps," she would say, "Go find a feather and catch that chicken over there for me."

I needed no further instructions. The procedure was routine. I'd look about the yard or henhouse for a dropped feather. One that came from a hen's tail feathers, slender and pliable, was best. By the time I had found the feather and cornered the chicken, which did not have strength enough to evade me, Mother would be waiting on the back steps with a pan of water. She would strip the feather to its rib up to the very tip, leaving less than half an inch; then she would rub the tip until it looked ragged. Now she was ready for the chicken.

"Hold the feather and give me the chicken," she instructed. She opened its bill, exposing the openings to the gullet and windpipe. Holding the bill open wide, she inserted the feather into the trachea, gave it a twist and withdrew it. Tangled in the feather tip would be a tiny red worm, less than half an inch in length. She dipped the feather into the water and dislodged the worm which wriggled about in the pan. Out of its natural environment, it would soon die. She released the chicken which ran off shaking its head and fluttering its ruffled feathers to recover, none the worse for its painful experience.

"There's another sick one over there. Catch it. I might as well take care of it too," she would say, and then repeat the procedure.

That was all there was to it. The chicken recovered and I was admonished again not to let the broods out until the dew had dried.

My mother did not know that the microscopic eggs of the parasitic gape-worm were carried in the droppings from the fowls to be picked up in the dew to complete its life cycle in the trachea or lungs of the host. She only knew that there was a connection between dew and "gaps" and how to treat the affliction.

Attending to the setting hens was another responsibility. Early in the spring Mother would watch for a hen that wanted to set. A broody hen would refuse to leave the nest, fluff her feathers, and squawk angrily if disturbed. Then Mother would select ten or twelve large eggs and place them under the hen. During the three-week incubation period, she sat patiently on the eggs for the entire time leaving the nest only briefly now and then. Nevertheless, I was required to place food and water in the coop for her, daily, until the eggs began to hatch. Then we kept a more careful watch.

A chick just out of the shell is a weak, pitiable little thing until it dries and gains strength. Not all the eggs hatched at the same time so we would remove the baby chicks as they hatched and take them to the house where they were covered with soft rags and kept warm. Hens often mashed the newly hatched babies if left with the unhatched eggs, so removing them was important. After several days, if there were unhatched eggs in the nest, we tested them to see if they had living chicks in them.

"Old Fussy Feathers still has three eggs left," I reported one day as I brought one baby into the warm kitchen. "She pecked me when I got this one, mean old thing!"

"Go get them and I'll see if they're going to hatch. Maybe they're rotten," said Mother.

When I returned she was waiting on the back steps with a pan of warm water. Gently, she placed the eggs in the water. Two floated. She took them and handed them to me. "Throw them away. Go over to the edge of the field because they'll smell terrible," she ordered. We both stared intently at the third egg. Inert, it lay on the bottom of the pan; then it moved, a gentle, barely perceptible motion at first, then a strong jerk.

"Put this back in the nest. It'll hatch by tomorrow; then we'll give Fussy Feathers all her chicks and she'll be happy." Mother smiled at me, and we both felt happy at having accomplished our purpose.

Back to the nest I went, cradling the still warm egg in my hand and finally slipping it under the disgruntled hen. Next day Fussy and her ten chicks set up housekeeping in a new coop under the walnut tree. Each morning, when I opened the coop, Fussy and her brood would hurry forth to begin their busy day looking for food. A mother hen scratches in the dirt and, finding a bug or worm, gives a call that brings all the chicks running. I had to feed them, too; at first a stiff dough made of corn meal and water was offered. As the chicks grew larger, they ate wheat and corn as well as insects and worms which they foraged for. As the season advanced, there would be five or six hatchings, timed to give us frying chickens throughout the summer.

When chickens reached one-and-a-half to two pounds in size, they were considered large enough to eat. A half dozen would be caught and shut up in a "fattening coop" to be fed and cleansed before use. As two or three would be killed for the table, more were added in the coop. All these lots of chickens and hens were my daily care; however, I often neglected my duties unless I was constantly reminded. Play appealed to me much more than work.

Marguerite and I loved to steal watermelons. They were there for the asking, but we made a game of approaching her father's patch or mine from a roundabout direction to make sure we weren't seen. Choosing as large a melon as we could carry, we placed it in the stream to cool.

Selecting a ripe one was something we did not know how to do at first. One summer it seemed that the melons would never get ripe. Impatient, I resorted to what I thought was a sure fire method. Borrowing a knife from the kitchen, I went to the patch where the melons lay green and inviting among the trailing vines. I studied several to see if I could tell which was ripe, thumping them as I had seen my father do and examining the curl. They all seemed alike to me so I carefully cut a one-inch cube from the top of a particularly big one. Prying it out wasn't easy, but when I did I could discern no pink flesh. Rats! I tried another — and another. One yielded a faintly pink tinge but when I tasted it it was not sweet. Thinking no harm had been done, I gave up.

A day or two later my father checked the watermelon patch to see if he could find any ripe ones. At dinner, the conversation was as usual. Daddy told Mother that coons were destroying much of the corn in the back field. "They climb up the stalk, pull off the shucks, and eat the kernels almost like a person," he said. I mentioned having found a hen nest in the carriage house with five eggs in it.

"You'd better try them to see if they are any good before you send them to the store," my father answered. Auntie reported that I had failed to water the chickens after breakfast. It was a normal meal.

When Daddy left the table, he called me to go with him. Unsuspecting, I followed happily, but, on the way to the barn, he stopped at a peach tree and pulled a sturdy little branch. My heart fell. I began to go over in my mind my various misdemeanors of the last few days, but I never thought of the visit to the watermelon patch. When he told me that I had destroyed a half-dozen luscious watermelons, I was shocked. Realizing that I did not know the seriousness of my act, he threw the switch away and took me to the patch. There he carefully pointed out the clues to ripeness: the drying curl, the yellow underside, the hollow thump. "Perhaps you'd better let me pick them for awhile yet," he said in conclusion. Though Marguerite and I continued to steal melons from time to time, I never plugged another one.

Summertime brought some eventful days such as wheat threshing, the protracted meetng at church, or a family gathering on July 4th, but the tenor of the days changed little from summer to summer. We continued to enjoy childish pursuits into adolescence. Childhood lasted longer then than today.

CHAPTER II

The Corn Crop

Corn was probably the most important crop raised on Tidewater Virginia farms. Its grain provided food for both people and animals, and its foliage and bi-products had other uses. Certainly it required more labor to produce than any other crop, but, in spite of this fact, farmers tilling only a few acres grew corn.

Spring plowing began in March or early April after the ground had thawed from winter freezes and had become soft and easy to turn over. My father would take a handful of earth in his fingers and crumble it to see if it was too wet to plow. Wet soil formed heavy, hard clods which resisted cultivation. If it was right, in his judgment, he would send Connie with Mac and Woodrow, hitched to the No. 11 Dixie plow, to the twenty acre front field to start breaking ground. If the day was particularly fine, he might hitch Nellie to the single-horse plow and begin the vegetable garden himself. He was avoiding my mother's frequent complaint that her garden was late because "John puts the field work ahead of everything else."

I liked to watch as the first furrows were turned. Connie would push the plow point into the earth with both hands on the handles and the lines to the horses dropped over his shoulders. When he was ready, he'd call out "Giddup," and the horses would strain forward to break the furrow. The first cut, dark and shining, lapped over the unbroken ground as he gripped the plow handles in his strong hands, the muscles of his forearms and shoulders bulging with the effort. To plow a straight furrow required skill. Connie fixed his eye on a tree on the opposite side of the field and headed for it, producing an even line of dark earth thrown to the right. On the return trip, he laid the next furrow neatly against the first. Clouds of birds soon arrived to search for worms and bugs. Hour after hour, the team worked: horses and man controlling nature through brute force and determination. Today I often wonder how these illiterate men could accomplish such feats of accuracy and design. They possessed a good eye, physical strength, and a desire to perform correctly that combined into an incredible skill. A man valued his ability to do a day's hard labor and ridiculed the shiftless ones who couldn't hold out.

Connie was a little bow-legged man who probably had had rickets as a child, but his chest and arm muscles were well-developed, and he was tough and uncomplaining. My father often said Connie could lift more than many men twice his size. His expression was one of perpetual good-humor. His wide lips covered white teeth which had never known a real tooth brush; he used a dogwood twig. A smile hovered around his mouth ready to spread at any moment. His dark eyes were keen and observant and saw things to do without his being told. He was gentle with animals, a trait that made him popular with my father and me. He was careful to see that a harness did not chafe and that the horses did not get overheated. He would stop to break sprays of indigo to put in their bridles when the mayflies were bad, and he had a gentle hand on the reins. He was also willing to do little jobs for me with no objection.

"Connie, would you move this bench for me?" I might ask or "Put the saddle on Woodrow, please. I can't reach across his back." (Woodrow was my favorite riding horse,) or "Turn this log up on end, please. I want it to be a table in my playhouse," and he would stop as he passed to help me.

"Connie humors Louise too much," Auntie often remarked. "John is paying him to work not wait on her," but my father would smile and say that he'd never miss the time.

My father and I had a very special relationship. I followed him everywhere I could, and he enjoyed teaching me to harness a buggy or saddle a horse. He even tried, unsuccessfully, to teach me to milk.

Charles, our other regular hand, had a personality totally unlike Connie's. He seldom smiled and took orders only from "Mis Shubank." He had no time to bring an armful of wood to the kitchen or to pump a bucket of water unless asked to do so by my father. I often slipped Connie a piece of cake, but I left Charles strictly alone. Perhaps I had a premonition of the trouble he was to cause and the deep hostility which I would feel toward him for years.

Spring plowing was followed by disking to break up the ground into fine particles. The disk was a heavy piece of machinery which had a row of sharp metal circles which sliced through the heavy clods turned over in plowing. This work was lighter for the horses since the soil offered less resistance to the blades. The purpose of disking was to render the soil more friable.

Harrowing came next. The harrow was a flat iron frame four feet wide with teeth set at right angles. It was dragged over the field to pulverize the soil further, and to produce a loose, loamy texture into which the grains of corn could be planted. After having gone over the field three times already, the farmer had to make still another preparatory step before actual planting could begin.

"Marking off" was really opening the rows for the grain. This was done with a six-foot flat, wooden or iron frame, similar to the harrow, except that the hoes were longer and spaced three feet apart. It opened two rows at a time, and into these little trenches the grains would be dropped by hand. Some farmers added another step by crossing the field in the opposite direction with the marker. This was called "checking." Where the two rows intersected, the corn would be planted. This method made it possible to work the crop from either direction: north to south or east to west. As labor became more expensive checking, as a practice, was abandoned.

While the fields were being prepared, the grain to be planted had to be selected and treated. A farmer usually planted corn from his own seed kept from the previous year. Sometimes he might buy a different variety from a neighbor, if he wanted to experiment a little. We grew white corn, as a rule, and chose tender ears for the table when it was at the milk stage. Special garden varieties were unknown to us; however, my father planted a couple of rows of popcorn in the garden for me. It could not be planted near the field corn or it would mix and spoil both. I never heard of popcorn being sold in stores until many years later. White corn could be ground for meal for our table and was fed to the stock as well. Yellow corn was said to be more nutritious for animals, but it readily cross-pollinated with the white and yielded a grain unfit, in my mother's opinion, for human use.

Uncle Combs, an ancient colored man in the neighborhood, was usually employed to select the seed corn and get it ready for planting. He had been a small child during the Civil War and his parents had belonged to my grandfather. When the slaves were freed, they continued to live in their cabin and worked for him for wages. In time, they bought a few acres of land and built a little two-room house. They raised a few vegetables, kept a cow, and cut enough firewood from our woods to keep warm in winter; but they depended on our family for employment. Uncle Combs still lived alone in this house about a mile away. Too old to work, he still needed to pick up a little money by doing odd jobs, and my father saved certain tasks for him. He expected

favors from us because, as he was fond of saying, "My
pappy and mammy uster 'long to y'all."

"Good morning, Uncle Combs. Ready to go to work?"
My father greeted him when he appeared at our door one
morning. (We used the prefix Uncle as a term of respect for
the elderly of the black community.)

"Near time to plant corn, ain't it?" he answered slyly.

"Ask him if he wants some breakfast," my mother
called from the kitchen when she realized who it was.

"Come in. We'll have some breakfast for you in a
minute. Then I'll tell you what I want you to do today," my
father told him.

Uncle Combs deposited an empty flour sack on the
porch, along with his shabby old hat, and shuffled into the
house behind my father. He took his seat at the kitchen
table, bowed his head, and mumbled a few words of
blessing before he ate.

"I want you to get me a bushel of seed corn today," my
father stated as they started toward the barn. "You can
leave your bag here now. I'll cut you a piece of bacon to take
home when you finish," he added.

Uncle Combs always carried the sack in expectation of
some contributions to his larder. In summer, he might get
some potatoes, cabbage or apples; at other times, perhaps
some meal or a piece of hog meat from the smokehouse. He
accepted any and all food gratefully, even though we knew
he expected it.

Uncle Combs climbed with some difficulty into the
grain barn, seated himself on an overturned bucket, and
began to pick through a large heap of corn. Seed corn was
taken from the best ears, large, well-filled ones from the
previous year's crop. Throwing to one side small or poorly
shaped ears, he soon had a pile of selects before him. Next
he shelled the small grains from the tips of the ears, his
dark hands rubbing the dry kernels from the cobs easily,
and threw them into a small bucket. At last he was ready to

shell the seed corn into a half-bushel measure held between his knees.

"You wants tar on this here corn, don't you?" he asked when my father looked into the barn just before noon.

"Yes, Uncle. There's a bucket of tar in the carriage shed. You can finish after dinner. Come to the house now and get something to eat."

Grinning broadly, the old man returned to the house for his second good meal of the day. Later he took the shelled corn to the shed, poured it into a large wooden box, and dribbled black tar over it, stirring it with a hoe to insure that each grain was coated with tar. The purpose of this treatment was to repel rodents and to keep crows from scratching up the grain and eating it before it sprouted.

Crows, considered to be among the most intelligent of birds, feasted on the newly planted corn. They came in flocks striding arrogantly up the rows and gorging themselves as if all of the labor of preparing the land and planting the corn had been done for their benefit. They were such a problem that farmers used various methods of scaring them off. A scarecrow was a common sight. Some were very roughly made: an upright pole driven into the ground and a crosspiece for arms, with a discarded hat on the top of the pole and an old shirt or coat on the arms. The figure was intended to look like a man and to frighten the birds away. The crows paid very little attention to this caricature after a few days, but even more elaborate figures fared no better. Some farmers kept a shotgun handy and blasted into the field to scare the birds who flew off but soon returned. Some even killed a crow and hung it from a stake driven into the ground in the field, a practice which had little effect. Tar on the corn made it unpalatable to the crows, but did not keep the grains from sprouting. Many farmers believed that tarring the seeds was the most effective protection against the hungry birds, so that it was a routine part of seed preparation.

Corn planting was not done until early May. A man took a bucket of treated seed in his left hand and walked down the marked row dropping three seeds into each hill. With his right foot, he pushed loose soil over the seeds, pressing it down lightly and moving on without breaking his stride to drop three seeds into the next hill two feet away. To an onlooker the man appeared to be following a stylized ritual, a kind of dance step with a pause and sweep of his right foot as he moved up and down the rows. A mechanical, horse-drawn corn planter eventually replaced the by-hand method. It speeded up the process and took some of the physical labor out of planting, but produced no better results.

Applying fertilizer was the next step in the laborious work of producing a corn crop. It was dropped by hand about two inches away from the hill. Often the workman fertilized two hills at a time depositing a handful on the left hand and one on the right as he walked between the rows.

As soon as the corn was up two or three inches, it had to be thinned to only two stalks in a hill. Young boys were often sent into the fields to do this. A farmer with several children in the family would not need to hire help. He even pressed girls into service occasionally, but field work was generally confined to boys, some as young as eight years old. A grown man worked for as little as a dollar a day so a youngster felt proud if he could earn fifteen or twenty cents. Thinning corn was not difficult, but the long hours in the sun, constantly stooping and bending, made it exhausting for anyone. A favorite remark among farmers was that this work required a strong back and a weak mind.

Often there would be missing hills in the field; either the grain had failed to germinate, worms had cut off the tender sprout, or crows had pulled it up, in spite of both tar and scarecrow. In this case, Connie or Charles would go into the field with a bucket of corn and a hoe to replant.

These plants would mature a little later but would be ready by harvest time.

After replanting and thinning, corn was cultivated twice. This was done with a walking cultivator drawn by a single horse, first when the corn was three or four inches high, and again when it was six or eight inches in height. Sometimes on a very hot day my mother would send Alice, or Mary, or whoever was helping her at the time, to the field with a bucket of water for the thirsty worker. I would go and stand with her at the end of a row waiting until he appeared and gulped down the fresh water, stopping only long enough to let the horse blow and to fan himself with his worn straw hat before disappearing into the green sea again.

In August, the farmers prepared to "throw dirt" and "to lay by." Using a single horse plow, my father or one of the hands went into the field and cast a furrow against the row of standing corn to the right; returning, he cast the furrow against the same row on the opposite side. Up and down between the tall stalks, he went until the furrow had been cast on both sides thus anchoring the plants more firmly in the earth as the tasseled tops reached for the sky and the ears on the stalk grew heavy. Sometimes wind storms blew over the tall plants and spoiled part of the crop. Throwing dirt helped to prevent such losses. When this final step in cultivation was completed, the crop was said to be "laid by."

Ridges between the corn rows were left after throwing dirt. A careful farmer then ran a cultivator over the balks to level them and sowed German clover seed. The small grains germinated in the loose soil and produced a cover crop which was plowed in the next spring to improve the land. Corn depleted the land; clover returned nitrogen to the soil.

Near the end of August or in early September, it was time to pull fodder. Extra hands were hired to augment the labor force for this job. Fodder was pulled while the blades were still green before they became tough and dry.

"Connie, you and Ned take the back field," my father told the men assembled by the well early one morning. "Charles and Sam will start in the field by the house. Don't make the bundles too big, or it will take too long to dry them," he instructed.

The men moved off to begin work as the sun rose over Uncle Rich's barn. My mother and I watched them go from the kitchen door.

"We'll have four hands to fix dinner for today," she told me. "Go pick up some apples and I'll see what I can find to cook in the garden."

Aunt Gay and our current company, Cousin Maggie and Aunt Lou, had washed the dishes and were ready to help with the vegetables when she returned. Dinner would be cooked early before the worst heat made the kitchen almost unbearable. Blinds were closed all over the house to keep out the blazing sun and render the rooms cool by comparison, but nothing could cool the kitchen when the fire in the range was hot enough to cook.

On my way to the orchard, I stopped to watch Sammie and Charles as they worked. Beginning with the first blade above the ear, they stripped the leaves to the bottom of the stalk. They used both hands and soon had a bundle which they tied with several blades and hung on the stalk beside the ear. The men, already wet with sweat, were racing, and even Charles was laughing and enjoying the competition. The bunches of fodder, dried in the sun, were eventually stored in the barn for winter feed.

At noon the men appeared at the house for dinner. No one owned a watch; they told time by the position of the sun directly overhead and probably by their gnawing stomachs as well. Hot, dusty, and dripping with sweat, they sprawled on the ground under the walnut tree's shade and rested a few minutes before rising to pump water for long drinks and to wash faces, hands, and heads. They filed into the kitchen to eat a heavy meal: cabbage, potatoes, shoulder meat, corn bread, and baked apples. The odor of sweaty bodies was almost overpowering, but the men seemed not to notice.

A week or so later, tops were cut. Carrying machete-like knives, the men invaded the fields again whacking off the tasseled heads just above the ears. The long tops were laid in piles between the rows to be gathered into teepee-like shocks to dry. The field of corn now had lost its beauty. The stalks, denuded of foliage, bearing an ear of corn and a bunch of fodder at a rakish angle, looked somewhat like a battalion of scarecrows left over from spring. Several weeks later, when the tops were dry, they were hauled to the barnyard and stacked around a pole to be convenient for feeding the stock.

The harvest, goal of the long days of labor and seemingly endless cycle of cultivation, began in late October or early November. The corn ears, by this time, were thoroughly dry and hanging in their pale covering of shucks ready for picking. Dark hands would snap them from the stalk and toss them into the wagon to be hauled to the barn for storage and shucked as needed. If the ears were stored before they were completely dry, the corn went through a heat and was ruined.

Another method of harvesting used by some farmers was to leave the entire crop to dry in the field, blade fodder, tops, and ears. Late in the fall, when it was all completely dry, the stalks would be cut off at the ground and stacked in the field to be hauled to the barn as needed. This practice was used mainly where storage space was limited. Hay for feed had to be stored in the barn. Corn, protected by its shucks, could withstand the weather.

Corn was staple feed for the animals. Horses would be given five or six ears in their feed boxes in the stalls, night and morning. Whole ears were thrown to the hogs, and milk cows received corn, too. Although hay and fodder were fed to the stock, corn was basic.

When shelled corn was needed, ears were fed into a corn sheller by hand. My father often called on me to feed the sheller while he turned the big handle. I pushed the corn into the chute and out would come the bare cob and the grain. We fed the barnyard fowls corn and wheat, and we needed shelled corn to make corn meal.

A staple of equal importance with flour, corn meal was ground at the same mill where we took our wheat. Meal served many purposes. Mixed with water, it became slop for the pigs, or a stiffer mixture was fed as dough to the chickens. Baked in large pans, it became bread for dogs and cats; no commercial dog or cat food was available in our area. Finally, it became a soft delicious batter bread made with eggs, buttermilk, and soda. No breakfast at our house was complete without this delectable concoction—truly a dish fit for the gods.

Almost nothing from the corn crop was wasted, from the cobs used for fuel to the shucks. Tough and long-lasting, corn shucks were popular for mats. The porches and kitchens of the well-to-do as well as of the poor displayed corn shuck mats for cleaning the shoes before people entered the house. The dirt would dry and could be shaken out leaving the mat clean and fresh-looking. The same tough shucks, dampened with water, were split and twisted into a cord used to flag chair bottoms. Shucks were even used sometimes to stuff bed ticking for a mattress.

Uncle Combs made corn shuck mats, a skill learned from his mother. He would appear with his bag, ask for shucks, and stuff it with all it would hold to work on in the long winter days.

"My mat is wearing out; I'll have to get Uncle Combs to make me another." This remark from Aunt Gay would result in a new one appearing on the porch before long. The old man charged only a dollar, and he needed money to buy coal oil for his lamp and sugar for his sassafras tea.

The activity of growing a corn crop spread over many months, from early spring until late fall. It required enormous labor, but as a life-sustaining crop it had no equal. Those who did not raise corn bought from those who did.

CHAPTER III

Making a Living

The economy of King and Queen County, since its earliest days, has been based on the land. Agriculture and forest-related industries provide the livelihood of the majority of its citizens today, as they did in the first decades of the century. Landowners worked their farms, had tenants, or farmed on shares. The doctor, the lawyer, and the county official usually owned a farm and supervised the growing of the crops, even if they did no work themselves. For others, who worked at some trade when their skill was in demand, farming was also a sideline.

The blacksmith, for instance, was in great demand until the automobile, the truck, and mechanized farm machinery made his skills obsolete. Horses had to be shod periodically, and the blacksmith made the nails and horseshoes and put them on. Farm equipment needed iron work: single trees, hames, wagon tongues, and buggy shafts had iron parts; wagon and buggy wheels had iron rims which needed repair at times. Trappers even had the smith make traps for them.

Andrew Revere had his shop at the top of Revere's Hill which we passed on the way to church. In the opposite direction at Contra, above Ino, Jim Brizendine operated another shop. On any given day, at either place, men could be seen in conversation, waiting, while the

28

blacksmith lighted his forge and hammered out a hook, a wheel rim, or a horseshoe.

Bricklaying was considered a skilled trade, but in the early 1900's, few brick edifices were being built. The bricklayer might run the chimney, but the house would be frame. He also farmed and picked up any work that he could.

Every community had a few men who qualified as carpenters, some more skilled than others. When my father needed a new shed or a roof put on a building, he might employ Ben Hundley. If the wheat thresher needed more repair than he and Uncle Rich could manage, they sent for Lieper Tuppence. None of these men could claim expertise; they did the best they could. Jack-of-all-trades, a term meaning a person who can do many things acceptably, could be applied to them. Lacking skilled workers, they came to each other's aid when needed. They were prompted as much by the spirit of neighborliness as by the prospect of a few dollars. Men often exchanged work, helping each other without pay, and expecting the favor to be returned in time.

The nearest stores were three miles away at Ino. One was run by Robert Smith; the other, by Byrd Courtney, who also was postmaster. Both were family owned and offered no employment for outsiders. They were general stores in the truest sense of the word; they carried a small quantity but a wide variety of stock: canned salmon, baking powder, coffee beans (all coffee had to be ground), yard goods, Vicks Salve, horse liniment, gum boots, nails, shotgun shells, coal oil, and candy. The candy was kept in a glass showcase which sat on the counter at about eye level for a six or eight-year old child. It was the chief attraction for me. When Mother gave me an egg to spend, I spent a long time deciding on which few pieces to buy, but always I bought at least one of the coconut cubes that I loved best.

The sign on Courtney's store read INo P.O. The lettering, a mistake the sign painter thought too unimportant to correct, remained for years. The name of the post office had once been Hollow Chestnut for a gigantic hollow chestnut tree that grew there, until postal officials requested a shorter name. The name chosen seems to have been a whim of the postmaster who was determined to go to the opposite extreme in finding one short enough.

The post office occupied a corner of the store and was separated from the public by a screen made of heavy-mesh wire. There were a few pigeon-holes for mail and a drawer for post office money. Patrons inquired for their mail and received it across the counter whenever they had any. Business consisted of selling two-cent stamps for letter mail and money orders. Mailing a package required great effort on the part of the postmaster who had to weigh it and decide how many stamps to put on it.

The mail carrier who served the post office usually rode horseback with the mail bag slung across his saddle as he traveled from Ino to Contra to Cumnor, a distance of possibly nine miles. When the mail order catalogues arrived, the mail became heavier, and the mail carrier would drive a road cart or, in bad weather, a buggy.

The Sears Roebuck Catalogue was a family "wish-book." Women and children pored over its pages studying the pictures of the various items and laboriously reading the descriptions. The women ordered clothing for the children, dresses, shoes, and hats for themselves (they made the family's undergarments). The men bought pants, jackets, and hunting or trapping equipment. Around Christmas, family orders became heavier as parents prepared for Santa Claus by ordering from the catalogue.

These mail orders were paid for with postal money orders. Few white families had checking accounts. They tended to distrust banks; furthermore, the nearest one was at least twenty miles away, much too inconvenient for deposits or other banking business. They depended on the time-honored cash or credit system. Some men paid their hands with due-bills which were honored by the store keepers until the employers settled up. If extra money was needed, a man sought out a neighbor with money to lend and gave him an I.O.U., paying back the loan a few dollars at a time.

Our community consisted of several farms within a radius of a few miles and a settlement of four or five colored families living on an acre or two of land which they had acquired through hard labor. Their homes were small, unpainted, cramped, and furnished with bare necessities only. Nevertheless, they deserved much credit for having made that much progress. The older members were approximately only fifty years out of slavery, illiterate, and unskilled. Most could neither read nor write, and the younger ones had only stayed in school for a year or two before being put out to work. These men had no form of transportation other than walking, so their opportunities for employment were limited to the neighborhood, where the farmers were struggling to make ends meet by hiring only when necessary.

A man with a large family was considered fortunate in some ways because, as the children reached ten or twelve years of age, he could put them out to work. Essex Gardiner and his wife Susan had a cabin swarming with little ones, and they were hard put to feed them when they were small.

"Uncle Essex, you ought to be getting along very well now," Aunt Gay remarked when she met him in the road one day. "How many children do you have out at work?"

"Lor', Miss Gay, I done los' count. Les'see now. Sammie wuks for Mis' Walden; Thomas, he over at Mis' Abrams; Connie wuks for ya'll. Louisa done married

Charles and libbing wid him. Viney and Evie, dey home,
but de's near big enuff to hire out soon." The old man
laughed happily. "Show heps a lot. Dat it do," he
concluded.

These boys were live-in help. They came to work at
sun-up on Monday morning during the busy season and
stayed until noon Saturday. They were housed, fed, and
paid $2.00 or $3.00 a week depending on their age and
usefulness. They were supposed to do light work: chop
wood, feed the horses, gather vegetables, run from the
barn to the field to the house, pump water, tie out the
cow, or any of dozens of jobs. They were "saving steps"
for an adult and gaining experience through which they
might in time become capable help. They certainly earned
their money, but they seldom saw any of it. When the
boy went home, his father pocketed the money. The
youngster really had had no opportunity to spend it. He
usually did not leave the farm all week, and there was
nothing to buy there.

Saturday afternoon, after the children out to work
had come home, was the time the colored people went to
the store. With a little money in their pockets they could
purchase a few groceries to supplement what they raised
at home. They seldom bought new clothes and accepted
used clothing with small regard for fit. In fact, they
looked upon the white people in the community as the
source of supply. Once my mother asked Uncle Essex if
he thought Aunt Susan would want to buy a hat for
which she might have asked 10 cents.

"Lor' Miss Kate," was the answer, "Susan got 'nuff
hats roun' home dere now to start a missionary shop."

The colored community helped each other in need.
When Hela's husband died and she and her three little
children had nowhere to go, her brothers, helped by
others, built her a log cabin on a half acre of scrub
timberland bought for a few dollars. They cut the trees

and used the logs to build the one-room house. Its dominant feature was a huge mud chimney which took up most of one side. The chimney was constructed over a frame, I suppose, to outline the size. Small bushes were stripped of leaves and woven closely over the frame; then it was covered thickly, inside and out, with clay mud which dried to a hard consistency. The cost of the cabin was practically nothing, having been made entirely of available free materials. Although the chimney looked a little like a gigantic dirt dauber's nest, it was functional. When passing, I always looked at it with interest, because it was the only log cabin or mud chimney I had ever seen. The men who constructed it must have been drawing on primitive methods remembered by Uncle Combs or some very old member of their group, for there was not another like it anywhere.

I never went inside the cabin, but I think Hela must have cooked over the open fire boiling potatoes or meat in an iron pot and baking ashcake on the hearth. The size of the chimney was so great it is doubtful that a stove could have been used with it, even if she had had money to buy one.

As the twentieth century advanced, a new source of income for unskilled workers appeared in the sawmill industry. By 1910, timber was beginning to attract businessmen from outside the state who could buy up rich timberland for from $3.00 to $5.00 per acre. Pine, oak, poplar, and gum, all abundant in tracts of standing timber, were in demand in northern markets. In the Ino community, Robbie and Bizzy (Bismarck) Wright, sons of Tom Wright, the highly respected colored preacher at Union Hope Church, began operating a sawmill. Garry Carlton from Essex County also began buying timber that offered employment to both black and white workers.

Up until this time, the men of the black community had been dependent almost exclusively upon farm labor for a livelihood. At the sawmill they were offered approximately the same wage, $1.00 a day, but there were variety and excitement in the new occupation. Men flocked to the sawmills, cutting back on the availability of farm labor.

When a mill moved into a tract of timber to begin cutting, the operator often constructed a shanty to house the men and to insure a convenient labor supply. He dug a well to provide water for the boiler of the steam engine and for the men and the oxen and mules needed in logging. The bunk house had bunk beds with straw-stuffed mattresses, and there was a cook shack where meals were cooked by one of the men. Plain fare such as side meat, beans, and cornbread, sometimes with dried prunes or canned peaches, kept the men happy.

The operation of the mill required a certain diversity of skills. Using a cross-cut saw, partners developed a special rhythm to fell the trees. In old growths of trees, men often tackled a giant two to three feet in diameter. Both stamina and skill were needed to bring it to the ground. Loggers, using mules or oxen, dragged the logs into piles and to the mill after the felled tree had been cut in sections. Handling a team of oxen required patience and understanding of animals. The mill itself needed a fireman to fire the boiler and get up a head of steam, and a log turner to get the log in position for the sawyer who pushed it against the circular saw to produce boards of varying widths and thicknesses. Others were needed to carry off the lumber, remove the sawdust, and remove the slabs. Finally the boards were run through an edger to cut them to exact size.

The slabs and strips from the edger were discarded as worthless, but they kept many a cook stove going and many a family warm in winter, at no cost except for hauling them away. The strips were particularly good for cook stoves since they had only to be cut to stove lengths, not split like the slabs or logs.

Other men were employed to haul the rough lumber to landings where it could be shipped to market. Wagons drawn by horses or mules hauled it to either the Rappahanock River or the Mattaponi, whichever was nearer to the mill; there it was loaded on two-masted vessels for the voyage up the Chesapeake Bay to Baltimore. Transportation by truck was not general until after the war.

Cutting railroad ties provided work during slack times, too. My father served as an agent for a lumber company buying ties. Men would go into the woods to locate suitable oak trees, fell them with the cross-cut saw, and cut the trunk into eight and one-half foot lengths. They were hewed with a broad axe on two sides and the bark was skinned from the exposed sides. The ties, scattered through the woods, had to be brought to the roadside to be accessible to the wagons hauling them to the river. They were snaked out with a horse, hitched to the tie, to drag it through the woods to the road. I went with my father sometimes while he tallied the ties and paid off the men.

At one time, shingle-making was a cottage industry along the Dragon where cypress trees were abundant. Tin roofs were in general use when I was a child, but many people, like us, needed a few shingles to patch old roofs. Uncle Combs liked to produce such shingles for my father when he needed them.

The old man required two men to saw down a tree and cut it into two-foot lengths; then he was on his own. He would square the cut sections, removing the bark with an axe; then he would split the block into thin pieces, six inches wide and one-half to three-fourth inches in thickness. A tool called a frow (froe), specially made by a blacksmith, was used for this purpose. It had a short handle set at a right angle to the blade, which was driven into the block of wood with a heavy blow on the thick upper side of the blade. The wood was split cleanly lengthwise; then the shingle was shaved to be slightly thinner at one end. Shingles were laid in rows; the second layer lapped over the first to form a watertight roof that would last for years.

White women had few opportunities to earn money. Housewives sold eggs and butter when they could spare them. Some, like Aunt Het, raised a flock of turkeys for sale. Our neighbor, Mrs. Carrie Moore, had apple trees and a cider mill; her vinegar was always good and for sale from her home as long as the supply lasted. Occupations for women included teaching school (until they married), taking in sewing, or operating a millinery shop. Colored women fared a little better. They did housework by the day and lived with their families; some young girls had live-in jobs by the week during the summer. Work was slow for everyone in the winter.

With the outbreak of World War I, changes, which had been taking place in the urban centers, towns, and even small villages, began to reach us. Some of the young men were called up, saw military service, realized that there was a world beyond our isolated community, and returned determined to join the twentieth century. For the blacks the change was even greater. Young men and women went north for jobs, returned with money, and encouraged others to join them.

"Where's Thomas working now?" my father asked Connie.

"Thomas, he gone out yonder," he replied, never one for detail.

"Well, I declare. I'm surprised. How did that happen?" my father continued.

"George Holmes 'suaded him to go back with him. They left Sad'day," Connie answered. George Holmes had been one of the first to leave and, in his periodic visits back to his old community, was credited with "tolling off" other young men.

"Well, I hope you don't plan to leave me. I don't know how I'd get along without you. How long have you been working here? Since you were a boy, I know. Must be ten years at least," said my father.

"Yes'suh, I 'spect hit more'n ten years. I hear 'em tell 'bout all 'dem houses piled on top o' each udder, all dem trains and cars and people. I scared of all dat. I qwine stay here." Connie had delivered a long speech for him, and my father was relieved. Connie was a good hand whom we trusted and needed.

"Out yonder" was the expression used by the local colored people for Baltimore, New Jersey, Philadelphia, or wherever, places they had never heard of and could not pronounce.

World War I brought changes to our community too, but they were gradual. Automobiles and trucks began to appear, and roads were improved. Wages increased at the sawmills and on the farms; schools began to consolidate, facilities improved, and new courses were added. Communication improved, and the way of life we had known became perceptibly different.

Making a living in the first decades of the century had required drawing on many sources to supplement a fluctuating income. People in rural communities recognized their interdependence; through buying and selling, trade and barter, exchange of labor and mutual concern for each other's welfare, they had eked out a living.

CHAPTER IV

Housekeeping

Man works from sun to sun
But woman's work is never done

This familiar jingle was literally true of the average farm wife. Her labors kept her busy from early morning until bedtime. The woman who worked outside the home was a rarity because the running of a household was a full-time job. Although labor was cheap and available, it was often unskilled and required constant supervision.

Keeping house involved more than the care of the house; there were the garden, the yard, and the poultry to be supervised. In some families the wife took over the greater part of these outside responsibilities; she worked the garden, gathered the vegetables, fed the hens, gathered the eggs, did the laundry, and kept things going indoors as well. My mother was never very strong so many of these duties were delegated to someone else, but she kept a sharp eye on those responsible for the work.

Perhaps the homemaker's first responsibility was to cook, for men depended upon and anticipate good meals. To provide these meals she had to know how to fire and operate her stove. The black iron range dominated the kitchen; it was a great improvement over open hearth, but it required skill to produce good meals on it. First, the homemaker must know how to build and keep up a fire. Wood for the stove had to be abundant, dry, easy to burn, and cut in small lengths to fit the firebox. This meant that someone had to procure the wood, cut it into proper lengths, split it into small pieces that would ignite quickly, and see that the wood box in the kitchen was kept filled. This responsibility belonged to my father, who either did it himself, or delegated it to the hired man. (One of my chores was to help bring in this wood because the pieces were not too heavy for me to handle.) Keeping the stove operating required regular cleaning. The wood ashes dropped into an ash box, which had to be removed, and emptied almost daily. To neglect this caused the fire to draw poorly. Across the top of the stove were six round eyes or lids which could be lifted out. Two were above the fire box and four were above the oven. From time to time those over the oven had to be removed and the top of the oven cleaned of a fine ash that settled there and served as unwanted insulation. If the biscuits did not brown quickly, it meant that this messy job had to be done. Below the oven was a similar space that had to be cleaned for food to brown on the bottom. Neglect these requirements and the food was poorly baked. My mother managed her stove with the skill of a professional, moving pots and pans from one part of the stove to another to receive the proper temperature and shifting positions in the oven to achieve the same thing. She knew how to add wood for a quick fire or to barely keep it burning when a slow oven was required.

Almost every item of food put on the table was produced from scratch. All our bread was homemade either from flour made from our own wheat or corn meal. Eggs, meat, and vegetables were from the farm as were the milk and butter. There were almost no short cuts to food preparation. To prepare breakfast took almost an hour. Two kinds of bread were always made, coffee was boiled in a coffee pot, and two tables had to be set, one in the dining room for us, and one in the kitchen for the help.

Milk and butter required an enormous amount of time. My father brought in two buckets of milk from cows milked by hand when he came to breakfast each morning. This was strained into gallon pans or bowls and set out for the cream to rise. The same thing took place at night. By the next day, a layer of cream would have risen on top of the milk. The cream was skimmed to make butter and the milk fed to the hogs. The cream had to be churned before it soured too much, or the butter would have an unpleasant flavor.

In most households in our area, the churn was a two or three gallon stoneware jar with a handmade wooden top or lid that fitted the churn securely. The dasher, also handmade, was a flat wooden circle with four one-inch holes evenly spaced around it; a handle about thirty inches long was fixed in the center. The handle passed through a larger hole in the lid. Churning meant sitting by the churn and working the dasher up and down with a rhythmical stroke, until little flecks of butter began to collect into larger pieces and gradually into a thick mass. Next, the buttermilk was poured into a pitcher for drinking or baking, and the butter was turned into a bowl to be washed with cool water to remove all the milk. A handmade cedar butter paddle was used to work the butter into a cohesive mass. This mass was salted and set aside until the next day when the salt would have drawn more water from it. Then it was worked again and any water poured off. Several workings were required to free the butter of all moisture. If not properly worked, it soon turned rancid and unpalatable. Butter was molded into a one-pound or half-pound round cake by pressing it into a wooden butter-mold. The mold was then inverted and the firm cake of butter was forced out on a plate. When milk was abundant, my mother would sell the surplus butter, sometimes for as much as twenty-five cents a pound. Her butter was always in demand because it kept well. In cold weather, when the butter hardened, working it over required real muscular effort, and in hot weather it became soft, oily and almost impossible to work. With no refrigeration, handling milk and butter in hot weather was very difficult.

Eggs, the housewife's currency, had to be gathered every day and sold quickly in hot weather. In extremely cold weather, care had to be exercised to keep the eggs from freezing.

Fowls provided a staple in the diet, but there was time-consuming preparation before fried chicken or roast fowl came to the table. The chicken was taken to the chopping block and its head cut off; then it was dipped in scalding water to loosen the feathers and then picked — by hand, of course. Killing a chicken was not for the squeamish. It was something neither my mother nor I could do.

"John, somebody will have to kill three chickens for me this morning before you go to work," she would say and my father would send Charles to get the chickens from the fattening coop. We always kept the chickens to be killed in a special coop to cleanse for a few days before using them for the table. The rationale was that fowls running loose on the yard would be eating indiscriminatingly and the meat might have a foreign flavor. One of my jobs was to feed the chickens in the "fattening coop" every morning. Their diet was a special dough made of corn meal and water and perhaps a handful of wheat.

Picking and cleaning the chickens were disagreeable jobs. The steam rising from the wet feathers had a nauseating odor, and opening the chicken and pulling out the entrails was nauseating also. The gizzard had to be split, turned wrong side out and the inner layer peeled off; the liver had a gall sac which had to be carefully removed; (if the sac broke the liver was ruined from the bitter flavor of the gall and had to be discarded); last the chicken had to be dismembered and cut into pieces for frying. The pieces were salted to stand for several hours before cooking.

I have seen my mother, when unexpected company came, send the hired girl to kill a chicken, dress it, and cook it before dinner could be served — an impossible task in the eyes of a modern housewife, I'm sure.

Preparing large fowls, such as geese or turkeys, was an even harder job. Some housewives saved goose feathers for pillows or feather beds, and the tail and wing feathers from turkeys were used for dusters. This practice was a carry-over from their upbringing and was not really necessary at this time.

Everyone in our community used oil lamps for lighting. Electricity did not reach us until almost mid-century when REA ran a line from Center Cross to Dragonville in 1947 or 1948. Caring for the lamps was a daily task. In the morning all were brought to the kitchen to be cleaned and prepared for use that night. The chimneys were removed, cleaned from soot with paper, washed in warm soapy water, and dried. A sudden gust of wind could cause the blaze to flare and smoke the chimney badly. The bowls were filled with oil, the wicks were trimmed, and the lamps were placed in a row on top of the cupboard. Like the wise virgins of the Bible, our lamps were ready. If oil in the oilcan was low, we knew that someone must go to the store before night or we would be in darkness. Oil was not produced on the farm; it had to be purchased.

Laundry was sent out each week to be done by a local woman. On Monday, the soiled clothes were put in the laundry basket along with some flour and two blocks of lye soap. Aunt Gay usually took the clothes to the washer woman. She loved to drive Mac or Woodrow the two or three miles to Clara's or Jane's or whoever was the current "wash-woman" with the basket in the foot of the buggy and with me beside her. It was a nice little outing on good days, and on bad days somebody else took the clothes.

Finding a good laundress was not always easy. Like many other household jobs, laundering required skill, patience, and hard work. In good weather most laundresses kindled a fire in the yard and boiled the white clothes in a large kettle. Then they were rinsed in clean water, put through a bluing water, and hung to dry. Some white things like tablecloths, pillow cases, and bureau scarves were starched before hanging. The flour sent with the clothes was mixed with water and cooked to a thick paste on the stove to make the starch. It was thinned to the proper consistency for different fabrics. Heavily soiled work clothes were also boiled, and shirts were starched.

Ironing was necessary for almost every piece of clothing. Mother expected the sheets to be ironed as nicely as other pieces. She would unpack the clean clothes, examine the sheets and say impatiently, "Look at this. Cat faces all over them," meaning there were wrinkles. Flat irons were heated on the stove; an iron was tested for proper heat with a moistened forefinger, and used until the heat lessened; then it was exchanged for another already on the stove. At least three irons were needed for a continuous operation. A hot fire was needed to heat the irons. In summer, ironing was a punishing, exhausting job. Washing machines, easy care fabrics, and electric irons have relieved the housewife of much of the drudgery of laundry. Clothing was changed as a rule once a week. It is easy to see why standards of cleanliness have changed so much when we consider the physical effort and time required then to wash and iron clothes.

Homemade soap was used for laundry, dishwashing, and cleaning. We bought soap for personal use. Mother saved grease from bacon, chicken fat, ham trimmings, or beef tallow, for fat of any kind could be used to make soap. When the supply on hand was running low, Mother would find a day to make a pot of soap. Fortunately, we could buy a can of Red Devil Lye, a great time saver over the older process of dripping lye from wood ashes, something I have never seen done.

The soap was made in a lard tin or ham boiler. About three quarts of water were added to one can of lye and stirred with a wooden stick. When the lye was completely dissolved the grease was added. The action of the lye dissolved the grease and, as it boiled, it thickened. The proper proportion of lye and grease was important; if too much lye was used, the soap would be strong and hard on the hands and on the articles laundered in it. Mother always kept the vinegar cruet handy in case some of it splashed on her hands. (Vinegar neutralizes lye.) When the mixture was thick enough, it was set aside to cool a little, poured into shallow pans and left to harden. Later she cut it into blocks and put it away for use during the next several months.

It is true that laundry soap was available for purchase at this time, but my mother, brought up during the period following the Civil War, was using skills learned as a girl when plantations were virtually self-sufficient. Using grease, which would have been wasted otherwise, seemed to her good management, not parsimony as were the many other small economies she practiced.

Visitors approaching Lewisville, our home, saw a white-washed frame building with a large exterior stacked chimney on the left. There was a high front porch reached by six steps which led into the front hall. Below, was the English basement (windows at ground level) which contained the dining room and a store room. The kitchen originally was in a separate building near the main house, but in my childhood, a single room had been added at ground level for the kitchen. We descended three steps into the dining room. A few years later we abandoned the basement dining room and built another, moving the kitchen back so that the house had a two-room addition to the side. There were seven rooms, not including the attic, which had to be kept clean according to my mother's exacting standards. She possessed few specialized tools; the broom, mop, dust cloth, and scrub bucket and rag were about all. A room in much use had to be swept twice a day, because the constant traffic in and outdoors brought in grit and trash. My mother, before sweeping, used the turkey wing as a brush to clean shelves, cupboards and tables of loose trash and dust. The kitchen floor was bare, unpainted boards kept at a sparkling brightness by scrubbing with fine sand. Jenny Bell was good at scrubbing and heavy cleaning, though unskilled in most jobs. She would sometimes ask me to find the sand for scrubbing, and she took great pride in the whiteness of the floors. I remember how pleased we all were when the first linoleum was put on the floor, partly for its bright colors and partly for ease in cleaning.

The time when cleaning reached its climax was the upheaval every spring. Beds were taken apart, washed and reassembled. Mattresses were dragged outside to be sunned and aired; quilts were washed before being stored. This was the time when feather beds were rotated with the summer mattresses, which were cooler. Making a feather bed was hard work, and it was a joy not to have this to do in summer. With the feather bed, the sheets had to be stripped back, the feather mattress turned from head to foot and beaten and shaken; then the process was repeated from side to side. This was done to fluff up the feathers and to give the bed a smooth, not lumpy, appearance. After this vigorous attack, the covering was replaced neatly and correctly. I had a hard time making a bed to suit Mother.

"It's a sight, Baby. You haven't half-way done it. Try to do better tomorrow." When feather beds ceased to be used I was happy indeed.

In winter we used quilts as bed covering. Mother and Auntie prized these handmade coverlets with their intricate patterns and bright colors and could identify the maker of each. One in the wedding ring pattern, made by my grandmother, Martha Walden, was my favorite. I loved too a blanket, hand woven of wool from sheep raised on the place and sewed together in three strips to form a large coverlet. Others were crazy quilts, the pieces sewed together in a random pattern, practical but not especially pretty.

I marvel at the accomplishments of my mother. Her standards were high and she took great pride in keeping a neat home and setting a good table. True she usually had help, but she directed the work, doing as much herself as anyone else. She believed that you must know how to do a task yourself to supervise others. She was on her feet from morning until after supper, and when she sat down, there would be mending, or darning socks.

Men's heavy work shoes quickly wore holes in their cotton socks, but no self-respecting housewife was ready to discard them. She darned them. She used a china nest-egg, or lacking one, she made do with a small dried gourd which she slipped into the heel or toe and placed under the hole. Using soft cotton darning thread and a large needle, she worked across the hole vertically, then from left to right to form a network. Skillfully done, darning restored the sock to comfortable usefulness.

She set a good table because she preserved and canned so many fruits and vegetables to supplement the winter diet. Her canned fruits included cherries, peaches, huckleberries, pears, and forty to fifty quarts of tomatoes. She seldom dried apples, though many people did.

Sewing was another of my mother's talents. She made her clothes, mine, and most of Aunt Gay's. I do not remember ever having a "ready-made" dress until I was in college. Mother attempted to teach me to sew but with little success.

As a beginning assignment, I was required to make two pairs of underpants, drawers we called them, for myself. Mother cut them from a durable cotton material and instructed me how to proceed. Three tucks, just above the hem, ornamented each leg of the garment.

"Put the tucks in first, space them the same distance apart, and keep them even. Use the tucker on the sewing machine, and let me see them after you finish," she told me.

I tried hard. I always wanted to please and, if I got it right the first time, the job would be over sooner. Inspection showed that she was not altogether pleased. She sighed and said I'd have to do better next time. The next step was to hem each leg. This was so simple, it was almost right.

"Now join the legs together, like this," she showed how the two parts joined at the center. "You are going to make a French seam so there will be no exposed raw edges, like this. See." She had stopped canning tomatoes in the kitchen to show me what to do next. "Maybe I'd better come with you."

"Oh, let her do it herself, Kate. Experience is the best teacher," Auntie interrupted. Back to the bedroom where the sewing machine, my longtime enemy, awaited! Half an hour later, I returned to the kitchen for the next inspection.

"Look, Mother, is this all right?"

Mother took her hands from the dishpan of scalded tomatoes that she was peeling, dried them, adjusted her glasses, took the half-made drawers, and looked at them closely.

"My darling baby, you have put them together wrong. See, one leg is wrong side out. Oh, Louise, how could you have made such a mistake? I pinned them for you first, didn't I?"

Crestfallen, I looked. Yes, on one leg the tucks and hem were on the outside, but on the other leg a series of stiches, not tucks, was visible.

"You'll have to pull it out. Take the scissors and rip the stitches carefully and don't cut the material. Bring it back here when you finish." She was exasperated.

"Rip it out." How often I heard that command! The sewing machine seemed to take perverse pleasure in misbehaving as soon as I touched it. Seam stitchings wobbled from side to side, the bobbin clogged, the needle came unthreaded; it was uphill all the way when I tried to sew. By the time the ripping was done, it was time for dinner and the sewing lesson was ended for that day, but my mother was nothing if not determined. "If at first you don't succeed, try, try again" was quoted to me on many occasions. I finished the two garments by summer's end and wore them too, but the project was filled with trial and error throughout.

"I'm afraid she'll never learn to sew," sighed my mother, and she was right.

I have purposely omitted an account of hog-killing, which was a major event in late fall, because I hated it. When the weather began to turn cold, I knew it was not far off. My father would say at breakfast, "It's nippy this morning. We had a hard frost last night. Should be able to kill hogs soon."

"Please try to get me some good help in the kitchen this year," my mother would answer. "Maybe Aunt Susan, Louisa, and Hallie would come. They're the best ones I know,"

"I'll speak to them right away then."

I hated the squeals of the poor pigs that I had helped to feed as they were caught for slaughter. I could not stand to see the man with the knife, knowing that he would slit their throats. I hated the thought of every step in the horrible undertaking. I would be awakened by the squealing one morning, and though I never went near the scene of operations, as I left for school I could smell the smoke from the fire burning under the big iron cauldron and could catch a glimpse of the steam from the water heating for the scalding. I would hurry off to catch the school wagon, glad that it was a school day and I could escape. Some children gladly stayed home from school for the exciting day, but fortunately my parents would not allow it.

Home that afternoon, I would see the row of pale, stiff bodies hanging from a pole. The spot where the tragedy had taken place was quiet now; the men were gone , their work done. Inside the kitchen, though, there would be a fever of activity: Viney trimming fat from the meat, lard boiling on the stove, a colander filled with cracklings dripping into a tin, Louisa grinding sausage, and my mother "up to her elbows" in it all.

In spite of my strong feeling about the process; however, I did not escape helping in the kitchen nor did it prevent my enjoying the fresh spare ribs, liver pudding, and sausage.

A routine event in farm families, hog killing provided most of the meat for the coming year. The man of the house was in charge of curing the meat using his own mixture of salt, black pepper, saltpeter, and molasses. Smoking was a time-honored method in use from colonial days. The practice was dying out in my childhood though many still used it. Our cured meat was hung in the smoke house, built in my grandfather's day, and no doubt the scene of smoking then, but my father produced delicious hams without the use of smoke.

Preparation of the other products of butchering fell to the women. First, it was important to make enough lard to supply the daily needs of bread-making and frying.

Fat was trimmed from the meat to be cured and from other parts of the hog, cut into small pieces and put in a larger kettle to be cooked. A small amount of water was added to keep the fat from burning. As it cooked, constantly stirred and watched by someone, it gradually was "rendered" to a clear liquid. When the bits of fat (cracklings) were brown and crisp and rose to the top, it was strained into tins to harden. Good lard was snowy white and tender with a low melting point. The cracklings were saved and used in making both cornbread and biscuits.

Sausage was made from strips of meat trimmed mainly from the hams and shoulders to give them a good shape. It was put through a hand-operated meat grinder, a strenuous task. My mother usually had the meat ground twice to produce a fine textured product with just the right proportion of fat and lean meat. She seasoned it with salt, black pepper, and sage and left it to stand overnight. Next morning we had fresh sausage for breakfast while she anxiously inquired if it needed more seasoning. This she would add, working the mass of raw meat with her hands. It was a disagreeable task because the mixture would be cold, stiff, and hard to handle.

The next step was to make cakes and fry them in big spiders (round, black iron frying pans) over a moderate fire. When properly cooked, they were packed in quart Mason jars with some of the fat added; the lid was screwed on; and, while still warm, the jar was inverted. This was the key to preventing spoilage. The grease hardened at the top to form an air-tight seal. (Sterilizing by the hot water bath came much later.) We enjoyed sausage until warm weather, when the grease would melt and the seal would be broken.

Another method in common use was to pack the raw sausage into skins or small bags, dip them in lard, and hang them in the smoke house to be smoked with the other meat.

Cleaning chitterlings (hog's intestines) was the most disagreeable of all jobs related to hog-killing, but one that many people did without complaint because fried chitterlings ("chidlin's") were considered a great delicacy. We usually gave them to the people helping with the slaughtering, and avoided that part of the operation.

Nothing but the squeal of the hog was allowed to go to waste. Liver and brains were usually used fresh, but the ears, snout, and feet were scalded, scraped and boiled. Pigs' feet were sometimes fried and served as a main dish, but usually the housewife pulled the meat from the bones, seasoned it, and made souse. This glutinous mass congealed when cold and could be sliced and fried or served cold with vinegar. The saying "always ready, like cold souse" is meaningful to anyone of this generation.

Salt fish provided some variety from a steady diet of pork. In the spring, we bought 100 herring to salt. They were scaled, cleaned, head and tail removed, and then split close to the backbone to lie flat. They were packed in a stoneware jar or tin between layers of salt which became a strong brine. Soaked in water overnight to remove some of the salt, and fried to a crisp golden brown, the fish made a delectable breakfast.

Friends of ours used a more sophisticated process which called for black molasses, brown sugar, red and black pepper, and salt. The fish were delicious and worth the additional trouble, but most of our neighbors, like us, used the simpler process.

Housekeeping was a full-time occupation which required many skills. The housewife needed energy, stamina, and pride to face the day to day drudgery.

CHAPTER V

Company

In summer, company was a constant presence at our house. My father's brothers and their families came for a few days every summer. Uncle Earnest, Aunt Eunice and their three children, Uncle Archie, Aunt Ruby and Susan, all lived in Richmond and could come by train to West Point and make their way from household to household. My mother's cousin, Ella Wise, with her step-daughter and small son, would spend a week or two. Cousin Maggie and Cousin Virgie thought a stay of three weeks rather short. Then there was poor old Aunt Lou, nobody's relative, but a lonely old lady who longed for country food and country ways, and who was happy to shell beans, peel apples, dry dishes, churn, or help with almost any task that didn't require strength or good eyesight. "Be nice to Aunt Lou," my mother would say. "She doesn't have many places to go, and she's a big help." Aunt Lou had no teeth and consequently could not enunciate very clearly. She took a lot of teasing from my father when she complained of the "dam weather," but she laughed with him. Sometimes a kindly friend at church would invite her to visit from one Sunday to another, especially when Mother had another crowd due, but Aunt Lou was a summer fixture for years.

Our house was known as the "home place," and this made it the center for visiting relatives. My grandfather

Walden had built it before the Civil War, in a hurry to move his ailing wife into it thinking her health would improve. It was half of what was known as a double house (a hall with a room on each side and a corresponding second floor). Slaves hewed the timber, made the bricks, dug the basement, carved the mantels, and constructed the lintels and window frames.

The first floor had a wide hall and a single large room to the left of the front door. This was the "chamber" which doubled as bedroom and sitting room. My grandmother's tester bed stood here with its canopy and dust ruffle. The space beneath, which in the beginning hid the trundle bed, usually had a few boxes hidden under it, and always near the foot reposed the large pink and white chamber pot. I remember when some visiting boys and girls and I were playing blind-man's-bluff and the blindfolded boy, groping around the bed, knocked the pot out into full view!

The second floor had two rooms: a large one with two double beds, and "the little room," an unheated one over the hall. The attic was floored and had plastered walls just as had the other rooms. The two rooms there had low ceilings and were used mainly for storage. It was a treasure trove of old clothes, broken toys, old magazines and trunks—a perfect playroom. It also provided sleeping quarters for Auntie and me when there was an overflow of company. It was not unusual for the three double beds on the second floor to be occupied with our guests.

The company I enjoyed most was the Tomlinson family. Cousin Irene, Cousin Will, and their children, Billy and Anne, always visited two weeks in August and sometimes longer. When the children were small, Cousin Irene brought a colored nurse with them, but as they grew older, we were free to range the farm in search of entertainment. Billy was six months older than I and Anne six months younger. We played in the barn, climbed

the ladder into the hayloft, explored the orchard looking.
for ripe apples, set up a play house under the big walnut
tree, rode the horses when we had a chance, and stayed
out of the grown folks way as much as possible.

The swamp was a favorite spot to play in also. We
loved the cool, shady, little grove of trees through which
ran the small, gurgling stream. At our approach, the little
green grass frogs leaped into the water, their long legs
making a flash of white, as they broke the surface later to
reappear as two big eyes and a blunt green snout. These
were our special delight. It took patience to wait until the
frog came up for air; it took speed to jump in and catch
him before he submerged again, and it took cunning too
because one of us had to approach from the rear so he
would be caught by surprise. With more experience in
such matters, I was the leader who gave orders.

"Stand still, Anne, you'll scare him. Do you see him,
Billy, over there by that bunch of ferns? Lean way over,
and you'll see him."

Billy would pounce, missing as often as he succeeded,
but by dinner time we would have three or four frogs
maybe more, in the large jar with a screwtop into which
we had punched holes to provide air. Back to the house
we would go, and after dinner we would sneak them into
the horse trough. This was strictly forbidden, but
spurred to disobedience by city cousins, I would turn the
poor frogs loose "to get some exercise" fully intending to
return them to the swamp before my father came back
from the fields at the end of the day. Sometimes however,
we would forget.

"Louise, I want to see you after supper," my father
said one night. His tone of voice caused instant alarm;
then I remembered. The frogs were still in the horse
trough! I caught Billy's eye, and he kicked Anne under the
table, being careful not to alert Cousin Irene. Their
mother was very strict, and we knew there would be

three whippings if she knew what we had been up to. Our behavior during the meal was exceptionally good. Anne ate all her vegetables, Billy did not ask for another piece of cake, and I was eager to bring hot bread from the kitchen without being asked. I even offered to dry dishes but, finally, Daddy caught my eye, nodded to me, and started for the barn. I followed repentant and full of excuses. "Daddy, I was going to put the frogs back in the pond and I forgot. Please don't whip me, Daddy."

"I'm sorry, Baby, but I told you not to do that. The horses won't drink from the trough when frogs are in it. I have to empty the trough and pump enough water to fill it. That takes time and effort, but worst of all, you've disobeyed me. I thought I could trust you."

"I'm sorry, Daddy. I won't do it anymore," I was weeping wildly.

"I promised you a whipping, and I must live up to my word," he said. His kind eyes looked hurt too.

The whipping was not very severe. I was more hurt because he was disappointed in me, than from the switch.

We were careful about the frogs for days afterwards, but one day I caught a very small one that we couldn't give up.

"Gus is too little to find his way back to his mother," said Anne. "We'll have to take him home and take care of him. Don't you think Gus is a good name for him, Billy? Look at those eyes. He's darling." Anne was always attracted to anything small. She loved baby chicks, ducks, kittens, pigs, and calves.

"Can't you find a bowl or something, Louise? We could raise him." For once Billy fell in with Anne's plan.

"There's the gold fish bowl. The fish died. I guess we could use that," I replied with enthusiasm. I was always ready to do what they wanted to do.

Home we went with the captive Gus. I secured the bowl without asking permission, and we put our frog in it and placed it in a cool spot under the back porch. We soon tired of this play and moved on to something else.

Early next morning, before breakfast, Anne's maternal feelings led her to the gold fish bowl. There was exhausted Gus, his eyes and snout out of the water and his legs paddling feebly to keep afloat.

"The poor thing is hungry. We must feed him right now," she announced. "What will he eat?"

"Flies. Frogs eat flies. I'll get the fly swatter and kill a fly for him," I was as filled with the spirit of a do-gooder as she.

Anne picked up the bowl and together we entered the house and proceeded to the dining room where Mother had the table set for ten. Orange-fleshed slices of cantaloupe were set before each plate. The tantalizing odor of sausage came from the kitchen. The rhythmic plop-plop of the pump handle could be heard from the well as Daddy pumped a bucket of water. A gallon and a half bowl of milk stood on the side-table ready for cream to be skimmed. Breakfast would be ready in a minute. We could hear voices as the crowd gathered. We would have to hurry to feed Gus before someone stopped us. Anne set the bowl on the table by the milk pan and took Gus in her hand. I stalked a fly with the fly swatter poised. Suddenly a gasp came from Anne. I heard a splash as Gus took a desperate leap into the pan of milk. We dived under the table as Mother returned with the cream skimmer and a pitcher.

Peeping from beneath the table, we saw Mother's astounded expression. What was that in the milk pan? She adjusted her glasses and looked closer. Two protruding eyes stared at her through a film of cream! Exasperated beyond control, she screamed.

"Louise! Come here this minute." Not a sound could be heard. Anne and I were afraid to breathe. Mother took the pan of milk and hurried to the kitchen. It would all have to go to feed the pigs. Fortunately, she had another, so there would be cream for coffee, but she was truly angry by now.

"Louise," she called again, her voice rising dangerously. "John, have you seen Louise?"

"No, what's the matter?" My father had entered the kitchen just in time to see her agitation. He stared at the pan of milk in disbelief, then broke into hearty laughter "Frogs! from the horse trough to the milk pan. What next!" There was no humor in the incident for my mother, however.

Anne and I escaped to the back yard and hid, but had to return sheepishly to the dining room when the threats of punishment became dire. Breakfast was late that morning because Cousin Irene took Anne back to the bedroom and administered a swift spanking. Mother sent me into her bedroom to sit in a chair for an hour, the most dreadful of all punishments for me. Laughter at our expense was loud and long around the breakfast table, and Gus was gone for good, poured into the bucket with the milk for the pigs.

Our interest in frogs waned considerably after that, but we found a new activity. The corn supply was getting low in the grain barn, and we decided to play there one rainy day, because there was plenty of room.

"Let's clean the barn for Cousin John," suggested Billy. "We can put the good corn over here, the corn cobs over there and sweep the place up to make it look nice." His face glowed at the thought of such altruism.

Marguerite had come over to play with us that day. The options for outdoor play were few, and so we all readily agreed. That is how we found the mice.

As we moved some corn, a mouse ran out and scampered away. Excitement mounted. Were there any others? We moved a few more ears and discovered a nest with babies. The nest was a mass of corn silk and shucks chewed to shreds and rolled into a ball. The babies were only a few days old, hairless, pink, with eyes still shut. They looked like three little pink worms. Anne was ecstatic.

"We'll take them to the house and fix them a nice, comfy nest, not like these old shucks, and we'll give them milk and raise them as pets, one for each of us," she babbled.

Marguerite immediately sensed an error in the arithmetic. "There aren't but three. I guess I don't get any." She was already miffed.

"Aw, Marguerite, we'll find another nest, but if we don't you can have mine." Billy wanted to keep peace.

Before we had finished our cleaning project, the farm bell rang for dinner and we trooped to the house with the infant mice hidden in Anne's pocket.

We took them to the attic and tended them faithfully the rest of the day, but the next morning they were all dead. This tragedy called for a funeral which we carried out without adult assistance. After all, some things are best kept to oneself.

One guest, who came at irregular intervals and whose welcome was never very cordial, was a fruit tree salesman named Gus Street. There were no public accommodations for travelers for miles, and farm families were usually willing to give a stranger a meal and a bed, but Mr. Street's visits had nothing to do with selling fruit trees—at least not with us. He never brought up the subject. He liked my mother's cooking and bed too, I suppose, because he would arrive early with plenty of time to make the next farm, and stay until after dinner next day sometimes.

Marguerite and I made fun of him. We mimicked his loping walk and his slow speech, even composed a little verse which we thought hilariously funny.

Gus Street, like the Jews,

Smell his feet, clean through his shoes.

Marguerite's mother wouldn't answer the door when he knocked, but my parents believed in turning no one away.

As summer ended and the relatives went back to the city, life became rather humdrum for me. My parents needed the rest after the busy summer, but I was sad.

I loved company.

CHAPTER VI

Going To Church

"Time to get up, Baby." My father stood at the foot of the bed reaching for my toe under the heavy quilt. He had made the fire in the heater as a special treat this morning. "Hurry, breakfast will be ready by the time you're dressed. It's Sunday, so don't waste time."

I snuggled down in the big feather bed and pulled the quilt over my head. I hated to put my feet on the cold floor, but there was no escape, and I did have to hurry.

I dressed by the stove, shivering as I put on the long underwear, pulling it on under the protective umbrella of my outing nightgown. The Saturday night bath meant fresh long drawers and shirt this morning. The water pitcher had ice in it, but I resolutely broke it and poured some of the icy water into the bowl to wash my face. I dressed in my dark blue box-pleated serge skirt and white middy blouse, my Sunday clothes. I pulled on white stockings and shiny, black patent leather shoes with white uppers, and buttoned the black buttons. My square red silk tie, which tied under the collar of the blouse, I took downstairs for Mother or Auntie to tie for me.

Things in the kitchen were in a bustle. Mother was cooking breakfast and Sunday dinner at the same time. She had been up since six o'clock, and it was now 7:30 a.m. A baking fowl, stuffed with her delicious mixture of crumbled bread, sage from the bush in the garden,

60

onions, butter, salt, and pepper, was in the oven along with a pan of tomatoes. A corn pudding was standing ready to be cooked. Mother was making a large batch of buttermilk biscuits. Some were for breakfast, the remainder for dinner and supper.

We hurried to the table in the dining room. My father asked the usual blessing:

"Lord, make us thankful for what we are about to receive. In Christ's name. Amen."

On the heater in the dining room, were four large bricks. We would wrap these in several layers of old towels and take them with us on the long drive to church to keep our feet warm.

After breakfast, my father went to the barn to harness Mac and Woodrow to the surrey for the six-mile drive. It took at least an hour if the roads were good. After heavy rains, there were mud puddles and heavy sand in places, and the horses could not trot for much of the way. Today the roads were hard-frozen, and we could make better time. Tying the team to the gate post, my father hastened to dress in his Sunday suit. Mother and Auntie had washed the breakfast dishes and were hurrying into their best clothes, too. By nine o'clock we were usually on our way. With lap robes and hot bricks we would be comfortable for most of the drive. There were three gates to be opened along the road. My job was to hop from the surrey, pull the heavy gate open, wait until the carriage had passed through, close the gate, and return to my seat beside my father. I felt proud to ride on the front seat and enjoyed the prominence of my task as gate-opener.

Neither my father nor I had any singing ability; however, we loved the hymns sung in church and often sang verse after verse for our own enjoyment.

"Shall we gather at the river, the beautiful, the beautiful river" was one of our favorites. Once having sung lustily for two miles or more, my mother, in desperation, spoke from the back seat, "John, that's enough. You and Louise have not hit the tune once in all this time."

We were members of Lower King and Queen, familiarly known as Wares. The oldest Baptist church in the county, it was organized in 1772. Prior to the Civil War, it had a large black membership which separated in 1869 to form Second Mt. Olive. The rectangular brick structure in which we worshipped was built in 1834. It burned in 1919 and was replaced with the present frame building.

The churchyard was well-filled with vehicles by the time we arrived. Surreys were few, buggies predominated, and sometimes a single-horse wagon would be there. People living within a mile or two walked. The horses were usually left hitched to the conveyances and tied to a tree to stand in the cold through the two-hour service.

We entered the church through a vestibule about four by six feet in size. On a stand to the right of the door, stood a wooden water bucket with a coconut shell dipper for the use of any thirsty members. Inside the sanctuary we found the crowd clustered around two large heavy wood heaters, their sides glowing red from the hot fire which the sexton had made that morning. We warmed our cold hands and spoke to everyone.

"Good morning, Mattie. Is Sis Leah any better?"

"How are you, Woodley? Cold enough for you?"

"How thick was the ice on the horse trough at your house this morning, George?" and so on—

The Sunday School superintendent opened the service with a hymn. My mother, who was organist, went to the organ and played the accompaniment with cold-stiffened fingers. At the opening bars of "Stand Up, Stand Up for Jesus" we rose and sang joyfully; my father and I, unaware of any discord, sang with the others.

There was an atmosphere of happiness. We were glad to be in church, glad to have fellowship with our neighbors, happy to greet each other, and have news of the week. There was pride that we were gathered in the house of the Lord on the Sabbath, as good Christians should be.

There were no separate Sunday School classrooooms. We had assigned places around the building. The Old Ladies Class occupied the area around the organ, the Men's Class had the Amen corner. My class met in the little gallery across the front, built originally for the colored members.

My Sunday School teacher, Cousin Mamie, asked each of the five little girls in her class to recite a Bible verse.

"Let the words of my mouth and the meditations of my heart be acceptable in thy sight, O Lord, my strength and my Redeemer," said Marguerite glibly. She looked around in triumph, knowing she would outdo us all.

"Blessed is the man that walketh not in the counsel of the ungodly, nor standeth in the way of sinners, nor sitteth in the seat of the scornful.

But his delight is in the law of the Lord and in his law doth he meditate day and night. Psalm 1:1-2." I recited my verses not daring to look at Marguerite for I knew I had made her angry.

"Very good, Louise," said Cousin Mamie. "Now, Geneva, let's hear yours." The teacher was careful to give everyone a chance.

When the collection was taken, each child untied a knot in her handkerchief and extracted a coin, usually a penny, sometimes a nickel, and placed it carefully in the plate. The total was seldom as much as 15 cents.

Sunday School, over, we reassembled in the sanctuary. The men sat on the right of the center aisle, the women and children on the left. This segregation was rigidly maintained; the only variation was for a newly married couple who might sit together self-consciously for the first Sunday or two. The honeymoon was over when they separated as an old married couple.

The pastor in his dark suit sat stiffly in the pulpit until time to announce the first hymn. The sermon was usually long and often boring, in my opinion, but the congregation listened attentively. From the amen corner at intervals would come a deep-throated "Amen, Brother" from a deacon or a pious visitor.

After church there was much conversation. The membership drew from an area of five or six miles in all directions from the church. Sunday services often provided the only contact many members had with each other. Invitations to Sunday dinner were extended, and little gifts were exchanged.

"I brought you some dried apples, Kate. You didn't dry any last fall, did you?" Mrs. Moore might ask.

"Here is a bottle of my cough syrup, Brother Billy. See if it won't help that cough," my mother might say, addressing her half-brother, W.O. Walden.

"Cousin Gay, don't leave until I give you the book you wanted." This from Cousin Mat Glenn.

"Pastor, won't you and Mrs. Loving go home with us to dinner. I've made sweet potato pudding which you enjoyed last time." Aunt Ella Eubank was famous for her pudding.

There was warmth, mutual concern, and shared moments before we dispersed for the long cold ride home.

The second Sunday of each month was "Communion Sunday." One of the deacons was responsible for providing the elements for the Lord's Supper, commemorating the last meal which Jesus shared with His disciples before he was betrayed.

The communion table was arranged before the sermon and covered with a white cloth. At the close of the preaching service, the deacons came forward and sat on the front bench. The pastor removed the cloth to reveal a tall silver flagon containing the wine, two matching goblets, and two silver plates. On each plate lay a small loaf of homemade "light bread."

After a prayer the deacons passed the plates of bread and each communicant, as it reached him, broke off a small piece and ate it. The goblets of wine were then passed along the rows. As each member received the cup, he took a sip and passed it on. At the conclusion of the ceremony, the congregation sang a verse of "Blest Be the Tie that Binds" as a benediction. The simple sacrament was observed with great solemnity and reverence.

Only baptized members of the congregation took communion. Occasionally a visitor of another denomination would be present, but he did not feel free to partake of this meal of remembrance. Even as a child, I was disturbed by this practice of "closed communion," long since abandoned. My father, in attempting to explain it, stressed the matter of baptism. "Baptists do not recognize any form of baptism but immersion," he said. "Jesus was baptized in this manner, and we follow his example." Although he loyally defended the practice, I believe he also questioned it in his heart.

In summer things were more exciting. Almost every Sunday there were visitors with one family or another. The congregation swelled tremendously. The windows were opened to the breeze, and to gnats, flies and mosquitoes. Children squirmed in uncomfortable shoes and starched dresses. Men perspired in wool suits (the same ones they wore in winter), and ladies fanned with palmleaf fans kept carefully from other summers.

I loved to go to church although it was the scene of many of my most difficult moments. I could never sit still and my wriggling and squirming embarrassed my mother when I was very small.

"Put her down, Kate, and let her play at your feet," said a neighbor. "She won't bother anyone."

Acting on this suggestion, Mother released me to play on the floor hidden by the high back of the bench. Not quite two, I found the opportunity of freedom most inviting. Before she could stop me, I toddled into the aisle and made for the pulpit where the preacher, in mid-sermon, took no notice of me. Not used to being ignored, I grasped his pants leg and stood beaming at the congregation. My mother was paralyzed with humiliation. Not for her life could she rise and bring me back to the seat. It remained for a young girl sitting in front of Mother to retrieve the adventurous child. She grasped me under my arms and lifted me so that all my clothes slipped up. Down the aisle we came, my mother always said in retelling the incident, "with Louise's bare stomach shining, her fat legs kicking, and the ruffles on her drawers in full view." It was one of life's darkest moments for her.

Another episode happened when I was five, and I should have known better. I had been dressed for church on this day in the annual revival in my very best frock. The bodice was hand embroidered, the skirt had insertions of lace and bands of embroidery, and a blue satin sash completed the dazzling outfit. I wore a bow of ribbon in my hair which matched the sash, and I may have been the envy of other little girls, but I was completely unaware of my finery.

After Mother had served her dinner, she looked around for her off-spring. She found me riding the pole of our surrey. The horses had been unhitched and I was gaily astride the pole, my sash untied, a smudge of grease on my skirt, and a switch in my hand with which I was driving the "pretend horses." Mother was horrified, but she went into action without hesitation. She confiscated my switch, turned it on me, and used it vigorously. The incident became one of her best stories.

Because I was such a restless child, my mother often took me from church, administered a little whipping, and returned to her seat, grim-faced and determined. She would see to it that I behaved or else. In spite of these incidents, I never lost my love for going to church.

The summer I was nine I "made a profession of faith." Most additions to the membership came from the nine-to-twelve age group. It was seldom that a person put off this important step until adulthood.

Baptisms were held on a Sunday afternoon during warm weather. There were no baptistries in rural churches; the river, a creek, or a pond, convenient to the church, provided sufficient water for the ceremony.

I was baptized in Uncle George Kerr's millpond. The pastor waded into the water at a shallow spot until he was waist deep. The boys and girls to be immersed, clad in white, followed hand in hand. When my turn came, he took my hands in one of his and looking up to heaven intoned the words:

"Louise Virginia Eubank, I baptize you in the name of the Father, Son, and Holy Ghost."

He then lowered my body into the water, keeping a hand under my shoulders. I closed my eyes, held my breath, and felt the cold water cover my head. In a moment it was over. Dripping, I struggled to the shore and the waiting arms of my mother who took me to a sheltered spot back on our surrey and helped me into dry clothes. As I left the water the next candidate took my place.

My father had been careful to explain the significance of the approaching ritual to me.

"You are following Jesus' example. He was baptized in the Jordan River. You see, Baby, immersion symbolizes the death of the old life. When you go under the water, your sins are washed away, and you become a new person, a Christian. Do you understand?" He looked at me, searching my face for a sign of understanding. I nodded solemnly, impressed by his serious manner and his tender tone.

I recall the event clearly. The open air setting is the natural place for such an experience. A hush lay over the pond, its quiet waters ringed by willows. The blue sky, the slanting rays of the afternoon sun, the faint scent of laurel blossoms and the soft singing of the crowd made a deep impression on me. The pond became the Jordan River, the church members became the witnessess at Jesus' baptism, and I felt a tremendous surge of emotion that this beautiful reenactment had happened to me. In my memory, the purity of that moment remains suspended, like a bubble in time, bright, beautiful, and serene.

The highlight of summer, however, for many people was the "protracted meeting," a week-long series of all-day revival services at the church. With us, it began always on the second Sunday in August. Farmers had a few days then after the wheat harvest and corn had been "laid-by" to take time away from the fields. The "tracted meeting" offered a welcome diversion for everyone.

A visiting minister would preach morning and after-noon throughout the week, a total of twelve sermons. He would be entertained in the home of a different family each night, be expected to eat dinner and a hearty breakfast the next morning, and be back at church ready for a day of preaching with energy undiminished. These revival speakers were men with phenomenal good health, enthusiasm, and endurance.

The morning service always began at 11:00 a.m. and ended sometime after noon depending upon how many extra hymns were sung when the invitation was given for lost souls to come forward. If one or two came, the preacher redoubled the strength of his appeal. The congregation would sing verse after verse of "Almost Persuaded," a hymn that ended with the refrain:

"Sad, sad the bitter wail
Almost, but lost."

This was the moment when some good sister was apt to "get happy." She would come into the aisle clapping her hands and shouting: "Praise the Lord."

While the fervor mounted, perspiring ladies fanned themselves vigorously, babies fretted, small boys squirmed, and hungry youngsters like me wondered how much longer before dinner. At last the morning service ended, and the crowd surged from the church and toward the dinner tables in the yard.

Here the ladies would be busily unpacking hampers, baskets, and boxes of food, all prepared early that morning. The tables, built for the occasion of rough lumber, were arranged under the trees back of the building. Covered now with an assortment of tablecloths, they were loaded with food. Each family had a few feet of space for its dinner; then another family laid out its display of food. Piles of fried chicken, plates of ham, occasionally a dish of lamb, and vegetables of every kind in season were spread in bountiful supply. The food was limited to what was raised on the farm, but it was provided in lavish quantity. I loved the corn pudding, butterbeans, and baked tomatoes. Like triplets, this trio always appeared together. If someone had a dish of sweet potatoes, early for August, other cooks were impressed and a bit envious. For dessert there were pies and cakes and now and then a freezer of ice cream.

The preachers were served first and bore away plates piled high with a serving from as many family dinners as possible, so as to slight no one. The exertions of the morning and the anticipated strenuous efforts of the afternoon, required prodigious quantities of food,

apparently. Guests were urged to the tables next, and the
home folks and children ate last.

Adolescents just becoming interested in the opposite
sex found the dinner hour exciting, as they tried to
attract each other's attention. For those a little older, it
was the ideal meeting ground. Couples with loaded plates
found a shady spot, sat on the grass, and ate, hardly
aware of what they were eating. More often than not, the
couple would sit together in church for the afternoon
sermon. Sometimes, however, they would have the
temerity to remain outside, the excuse being that they
couldn't find a seat.

The dinner hour was a truly social occasion for older
people as well. Visiting relatives caught up on family
news, children were rounded up to be introduced to
comments such as: "He's the spitting image of Uncle
Ned," or, "Who does she take after?" Often they transferred baggage and went home with another cousin for a
few days' visit.

Knowing they would be back at church the next day,
children petitioned parents to be allowed to spend the
night with a friend. I always looked forward to spending a
night with Frances or Ella or having them home with me.

The afternoon service began when strains of the
organ reached the ears of the people outside, and they
streamed back to find seats near a window if possible. No
electric fans or air conditioning alleviated the August
heat. Late comers had to take conspicuous places near the
front. I dared not remain outside as some younsters did,
much as I would have liked to. At each service my
mother's eyes roved the congregation until she found me,
and I knew that punishment would be inevitable if I tried
to skip. Long ago I had found that I could not bluff.

"What did the preacher preach about this afternoon,
Louise?"

"The prodigal son."

"No, that was this morning. What was the sermon on this afternoon?"

"The feeding of the five thousand, wasn't it?"

"No. You weren't in church this afternoon, were you? I never saw you."

"I was sitting behind Cousin Lulie Smith, Mother. She is so big she just hid me, and that blue hat of hers is so big it would hide two people."

"Don't tell me a story, Louise. I'll just have to give you two whippings." Mother was regretful but determined, and I knew it. I knew better than to stay outside after having tried it once.

We dressed in our best clothes for these occasions. One summer I had a yellow organdy dress which I thought was beautiful. Seated in the amen corner one afternoon, wedged between Marguerite and Frances, I felt a strange sensation along my leg. I held my breath and waited. Suddenly a big grasshopper emerged from a fold of my petticoat. I grabbed him through the sheer organdy in a death grip. Marguerite giggled; Frances snickered. Across the church I saw my mother's gaze fixed on me. She knew something was wrong but not what. Afraid to blink, I gazed at the preacher as though entranced, while I grasped the grasshopper and my dress in a vise-like hold. Through the endless sermon I sat afraid to let go, afraid I'd ruined my dress, afraid I would laugh, and hating Marguerite and Frances for their amused glances. Their mothers seemed quite unconcerned about their behavior.

At the close of the service when we stood up to sing, I opened my hand. A dead grasshopper, squashed to a pulp, fell to the floor and an ugly brown stain marred my lovely dress.

As revival week ended, there were mixed feelings among different age groups. I was glad it was over. Every afternoon we had hurried home from church to begin preparations for the next day's dinner.

"You pick butterbeans first, Baby. Then I want you to get some apples from the tree behind the barn," my mother would say to me, and to Auntie, she would say, "Sister you make a cake before I have to fix supper." Like a drill sergeant, Mother assigned our jobs, and off we went to carry them out.

"Haven't you got enough beans yet? Hurry up. Go tell Daddy I need a dozen ears of corn." Her call seemed to come in no time at all.

We were all kept running. No food could be cooked until next morning because of the lack of refrigeration. Our icehouse provided ice for beverages but not any to put in an icebox. Next morning we were up by five o'clock to kill, pick, and fry chickens, make biscuits, cook vegetables, and pack up the dinner. The drive to church took an hour, morning and afternoon, and when we got home my father had barn work to do, cows to milk, stock to feed, and wood to get for the cookstove. There was no lightening of the work.

I wondered at my parent's willingness to go through this annual event cheerfully, and even to look forward to it.

The "protracted meeting" served more than one purpose. Social contacts were needed as much as the opportunity for religious and emotional outlets. It was also a meeting ground for all classes in the community. People knew and respected each other because they met and worked together through the church.

CHAPTER VII

School Days

Public education in Virginia dates from the Education Act of 1870, but from the first, progress was slow due to both poverty and prejudice. By the turn of the century, graded schools and high schools were well-established in the cities and towns; however, in rural areas the situation had not progressed so far. The state was dotted with small one and two-teacher units. In our area there were several one-room schools serving the children within walking distance of each. The age levels often ranged from five or six-year olds learning their letters, to boys and girls of twelve or thirteen, some of whom might be studying algebra or Latin. The teacher was supposed to be proficient in all subjects. The era of the one-room school continued in many isolated areas of the state into the 1930's.

I entered Carlton's Store School as a beginning pupil in 1914 under Aunt Gay, who was completing her thirtieth year of teaching and would retire at the end of the session. The school was more than five miles from our home, further than she wished to drive each day, so she rented a room from a family living near the school and "room-kept."

This meant that Auntie prepared our meals on the wood stove in the room in which we slept. Since she arrived at school on Monday mornings and returned home on Fridays, and since she brought much food from home, the housekeeping was not very arduous. Auntie's interests were decidely more intellectual than domestic. I found the arrangement a novelty and loved it, I suppose because Auntie allowed me to do pretty much to suit myself.

The school was typical of single-teacher units. It was a frame building about 30 x 20 ft. with a hip roof and a heavy door at the front. At the opposite end, a platform about twelve inches high extended across the width of the room. On it, stood the teacher's desk and chair, and a blackboard covered half of the wall behind it. The pupils' desks were handmade to accommodate four or five children. The top slanted so that anything put on it slid off into the student's lap or on the floor. The backs were high with a rail that hit the spine in a most disagreeable way. Definitely they were not made for comfort.

The central feature of the room was the large cast-iron stove which stood in a box of sand. A safety measure, the sand box caught the live coals which often fell from the stove when it was being stoked. Fire wood was kept stacked in back of the building. It was the responsibility of the teacher to see that it was cut into stove lengths and brought in daily. She kindled the fire each morning when she arrived, but she assigned the duty of splitting wood and preparing kindling for fire-building to the older boys among the pupils. From time to time, ashes had to be removed and the stove polished. Sweeping the building was also the teacher's duty, but older girls were always willing to do this chore. There was no janitor.

School opened in October for a six-month term because farmers needed their children to help with the work at home. Nevertheless, attendance was poor until crops were harvested and cold weather set in. There was no public transportation; everyone walked to school. On rainy days, only the hardiest pupils or those living quite near attended. A big snow storm might close the school for days.

A school teacher, though looked up to and respected in the community, received a very meager salary. Aunt Gay ended her thirty-year career with a pay-check of $22.50 per month. Her pension after retirement was a quarterly payment of $30.00.

There was one other beginner the year I entered, and Dot Williams and I had an enviable position: pets of the school. The big boys and girls did the chores while we were watched over, protected, and admired. School was a breeze.

At big recess, as we called it, we ate lunch and hurried outside to play in the schoolyard if the weather was good. There was, of course, no planned recreational program, no real playground, and no equipment. We were strictly on our own as to how we spent our time. We played "prisoner's base," "run, sheep, run," "gully, gully keeper," and "crack the whip," all games in which any number could take part. One of our favorites was "Annie, over," played when someone brought a ball to school. In this game we divided into two groups; one took the left side of the building, the other the right. The object of the game was to toss the ball over the roof to be caught or picked up by the waiting group who then raced around the building and tagged one on that side. This player was out and had to watch until a new game started. The game continued with the play reversing after each toss. The name came from the call "Annie" from the side with the ball to which the reply was "Over" from the opposing group as the play began.

It was an active, busy game, good for crisp fall days, and neither age nor gender mattered. When, at the end of recess, the teacher came to the door and and rang the brass handbell, that always stood on her desk, we returned to work breathless and good-humored after vigorous play.

Sometimes, we would venture into the woods back of school in search of foxgrapes or chinquapins. On one of these occasions, the big boys taught Dot and me to ride a sapling. One would climb a slender little tree, like a red gum, going as far up as possible before it began to bend under his weight. Then willing hands would catch the top and pull it to the ground and hold it until Dot or I took the position of the heavier boy. Released, the tree would spring into the air giving us an exhilarating ride. As the tree began to bend again someone would jump and grab a branch to bring it down for a second rider.

Daring. Risky. A little crazy. But I do not recall that anyone was ever hurt.

Although school was not all play, I do not remember learning to read; probably I had learned before I started to school. That year Dot and I progressed rapidly going through the first, second, and third readers. Arithmetic apparently did not receive much emphasis. I do remember having a slate and pencil on which Auntie would put exercises for me to work with, such as $2 + 2$, $4 - 2$, $6 + 3$. It was incredibly easy. At the end of the session, I was considered ready for fourth grade, inasmuch as I had finished the third reader.

The following year, after Aunt Gay's retirement, she taught me at home. This seemed a perfectly reasonable arrangement to my parents. My mother had been taught by a tutor first in her own home. Later, she had attended private school in her half-brother's home with his children. My aunt had an excellent reputation as a teacher, so what could be more suitable. Too young to walk three miles to Hollow Chestnut School or to drive a horse alone, I was indeed fortunate, so my parents thought, to receive schooling at home. My father built a little low table for my use and I suppose that we had lessons regularly, but I have no recollections of them now.

The big change came the following year. Realizing that I was not receiving a proper education, my parents arranged for me to board with relatives living in Urbanna where there was a thriving school. Cousin Carl Tomlinson and his wife, Pearl, a young couple who had no children, readily accepted the responsibility of taking care of me. Not quite ten years old, I left home for the first time to enter an entirely different world.

School began in late September, earlier than the one-room units, because the students were not farm boys and girls needed to help with the farm work. On the day that school opened, Aunt Gay went with me to enroll. Since I had no report card to show my grade placement, a consultation with the principal took place. Auntie produced some of my composition work, and I was asked to read. Favorably impressed, the principal placed me in the fifth grade. At that time I had had only one year of actual school attendance!

The school itself was a splendid two-story brick building, with six classrooms and a large auditorium on the second floor. There were seven grades and a four-year high school. The enrollment, small by today's standards, seemed enormous to me. When the bell rang, the pupils lined up in front of the building and the principal, a heavy-set man with a black mustache, ordered them by lines into the building. Overawed by such formality, I was uncomfortable and ill-at-ease.

My teacher, Miss Northern, taught fifth and sixth grades in a self-contained classroom, not unlike the one-room version I was accustomed to, except that we had only two grades instead of six or seven. I returned home loaded with books at the end of the first day. They were language, Virginia history, geography, physiology and hygiene, a Locker writing book, and a forbidding brown book, *Smith's Arithmetic,* which I distrusted on sight.

This was a time of many adjustments for me. Not only was I attempting to cope with separation from my parents, with living under different family arrangements, and with becoming used to a large school body, but also I was being introduced to organized instruction and homework. I came home each afternoon with assignments in all subjects, which I tackled manfully.

History and geography were delightful; language and hygiene were easy; but I found arithmetic a nightmare. I probably knew the multiplication tables, but I was unprepared for problems. My powers of reasoning had not been developed to deal with the complicated situations presented nightly for my solution. The fact that I did not fail arithmetic was due entirely to Cousin Pearl. I was expected to do my homework while she was preparing supper. Faced with a page of problems, I promptly froze. I knew I was over my head, but for some reason, no one seemed ever to have thought of placing me in a lower grade. I'm sure I would have fought the idea like a tiger. I had my share of pride, and I felt that I could make up for my poor preparation, given time. As it was, my self-confidence was severely damaged, and I suffered in silence and shame. I struggled valiantly with the arithmetic problems each evening. I would read the first one, then finding that I hadn't the foggiest notion of how to begin, I would gather my book, tablet, and pencil and clump down the hall to the kitchen.

"Cousin Pearl, could you help me with this one?" I tried to give the impressions that this was the only one that stumped me.

"Let me see it." She would, perhaps, be making biscuits and would dust the flour from her hands, stoop down beside me, and read the problem.

"A man in Buffalo takes train A for Albany. A man in Albany takes train B for Buffalo. If train A is traveling at the rate of 60 miles an hour, the distance between the cities is 107 miles, etc, etc, etc."

In a few minutes she would work the baffling thing, and I would return to the living room, where I was studying, to read the second problem. Equally unable to cope with No. 2, I would, after a decent interval, return to the kitchen for help again.

Cousin Pearl was patient and willing to help. She was probably amused at my poor performance, but she never failed to respond to my pleas.

We worked long complicated problems in partial payments or compound interest that covered a whole page. I attempted to determine how much paper would be needed to paper a room, allowing for window and door openings, and with her help solved that mystery. Together we plastered and carpeted rooms. It was revolting stuff. The most irritating type was the problem in which a boy seated on the bank of a stream has to find the height of a tree. I could have found pleasure in climbing the tree, dropping a plumb line from its top, and then measuring the line. There was drama and excitement in such a solution, but pencil and paper? How dull! How boring! How incomprehensible!

Figures intimidated me. I despised their rigidity. I liked room for fantasy, for enrichment, for flavor, and variety. What could you do with figures? Inflexible, arrogant, annoying things! They were as alike as bumble bees.

But words were different. I responded to the beauty of language; poetry and descriptions thrilled me with mental pictures of color and variety. Narratives had the power to inform, to excite, to sadden, or to create suspense. Reading made me a richer person. Words were the building blocks of infinite entertainment.

From Auntie, I had acquired my love for reading. All her life a lover of books, she would sit engrossed for hours, take the book to bed with her, and read far into the night. She would rise the next morning with a headache, too sick to help with the housework, but able to follow the absorbing book to the end. She encouraged me to read, bought books for me, and praised my ability. Perhaps the debt I owe her for this cancels out the trauma of arithmetic.

In Urbanna I found books to read that I took to bed with me and read after the lights should have been out. I hid my book carefully under the mattress and kept up this delightful occupation for months before it was discovered.

At Christmas my favorite gifts were always books. One year, someone gave me a copy of *Swiss Family Robinson* by Johann Wyss which I found fascinating. I read it every year—five or six times at least—and enjoyed it equally each time. At ten or eleven, I was reading the Little Pepper books, the Bobbsey Twins, Horatio Alger books, and *Little Women* and others by Alcott. By the time I entered eighth grade, Scott and Dickens were my favorites. I particularly enjoyed historical novels, and thought *Scottish Chiefs* by Jane Porter was one of the best.

The summer that I broke my arm, Cousin Kate Eubank brought me a set of Elsie Dinsmore books—eight or ten in the series, I think. I devoured them all, though, it would be impossible to find a heroine more unlike me than the saccharin-sweet Elsie. I wept with her through all her many trials and admired her sincerely, though I never tried to emulate her. My model was more the tomboy Jo in *Little Women*.

It was during my stay in Urbanna that I saw my first airplane close up. As World War I dragged on, biplanes were seen flying at great heights fairly often. At first I would run to the door when I heard the far off drone of the motors, I would locate the speck in the skies and watch it until it disappeared, but by 1918 they had become commonplace. However, one spring day when all the schoolroom windows were up, pupils heard the roar of a motor overhead. We rushed to the windows to see a plane thundering by, almost brushing the trees. It was obvious that it was coming down! No one thought of asking permission; everyone made a mad dash for the door, rushing wildly outside and across the fields in the direction the plane was headed. The principal tried to stop us, but his cries of "Come back. Come back," were completely ineffectual. The entire school streamed forward, each person frantic to reach the scene first. We arrived to find the single motor biplane on the ground and the pilot climbing unhurt from the cockpit. Wearing an army uniform, helmet and goggles, he seemed to the excited children to be an Olympian god just descended from the skies. He explained that his plane was in need of gas and asked for directions to a telephone. Townspeople began to arrive to offer help, and our principal, who had caught up with his runaway pupils by then, ordered everyone to return to school. The wonderful event was over. Back in class, we could talk of nothing but the plane. We had really seen one on the ground. Some had even touched it, and the pilot, as we described him, became a glorious, almost superhuman figure.

While I was in Urbanna, I began taking music lessons. Although my mother was an accomplished musician, she had thought it better that someone else start me. I found five-finger exercises boring, and counting and time were equally disagreeable. I had 30-minute practice periods twice a week which seemed endless. I spent much of the time rising from the piano stool to consult the clock in the next room. I took music for several years thereafter, but finally Mother realized that it was futile. Another disappointment. I would not be a musician.

At last, the consolidation of small school units into larger, comprehensive ones was reaching our area. A new school, similar to the one in Urbanna, was being built at Center Cross, and the children from my neighborhood were to attend it. The little one-room building, where the adults of the community had learned to read, was to be closed. Public transportation would be provided for the first time. Great was the rejoicing! I could live at home and go to school, so plans were made for me to enter the new school in the fall.

I left Urbanna with some regret. I had made friends, and I had found living in town an interesting experience. Houses were close together, playmates lived across the street, stores and churches were near, and I loved the street lights and church bells. Two Hupmobiles and a Cadillac were often seen on the streets, and there was even a telephone in the town. But I had never liked the hard pavements, so unlike the soft dirt paths I knew at home. I had missed my pets and the freedom of the wide playground that I had enjoyed on the farm, to say nothing of the homesickness I had endured. Of course, I was glad to go home.

Opening day at the new school saw the children of our small King and Queen community arriving in a strange conveyance. The contract to transport the pupils had been let to Cell Young, but apparently there had been no provisions as to the kind of vehicle. He provided a one-horse spring wagon, had a carpenter build seats down each side and across the front, and had a blacksmith to make several iron hoops to form a framework over which he stretched white canvas for a cover. It resembled a lop-sided miniature Conestoga wagon—a laughable affair. It created a small sensation among the other vehicles already at the school. There were two buses, (really trucks with a body built to provide seats down each side), and a number of horse-drawn conveyances, but ours was unique. It soon earned the sobriquet of "The Ino

Express" which clung to it long after its appearance improved.

This group of new pupils felt like fish out-of-water in the new environment, but I was not as overwhelmed by this change as I was by the one to Urbanna. However, I could sympathize with the others.

At home that afternoon, there were many questions about how my day had been, but the real discussion took place around the supper table after my father had finished his labors for the day and was ready to listen. He was especially interested in the ride to school.

"How was the trip this morning, Baby?"

"Everybody laughed at us when we drove into the yard in that old wagon. They called us 'country hicks'," I answered.

"Sticks and stones may break my bones but names will never hurt me," quoted Aunt Gay who was always ready with a proverb to suit the occasion.

"We were late too. I hated to walk into that room full of strange people and late," I continued.

"Why did it take so long, Louise? It's only six miles," said my father.

"Well, that poor old horse couldn't pull the wagon through the sand bar after we crossed Bird's Bridge, so I suggested that we get out and walk. It was better than that bumpy old wagon. We didn't get back in until the top of Newbill's hill. I guess we didn't walk fast enough. Clarence and Lee found a tree covered with foxgrapes and picked some for me. Mr. Young didn't mind," I replied importantly.

"I know your shoes were a sight by the time you got to school. Did you get grape stains on your dress?" Mother had taken pains with my appearance for the first day, and she had a mental picture of the way I looked on arrival that did us no credit.

"Well, I sat on a bunch after I got back in the wagon, but I washed that place out at school. It doesn't show much."

"My goodness! I'll see what I can do after supper." She looked annoyed.

"I don't like your getting to school late. Mr. Young will have to use a double team. I'll speak to him," grumbled my father.

"No, he can't. It's a single-horse wagon," I pointed out.

There was gloom around the table. The "public transportation" so long anticipated was not to be the perfect solution to my school attendance problems after all.

The next morning, however, my father drove me to catch the wagon and had a talk with the driver who insisted that he would not be late again. The wagon left each morning at 7:30 a.m. and did indeed arrive on time some mornings. The return trip put me home about 5:00 p.m. As the days grew shorter my parents became more and more dissatisfied. It was almost dark by the time I reached my house, and I left in the early morning light. Finally, after Thanksgiving, they found a boarding place for me in sight of the school. I did not ride the wagon again until the days lengthened in the spring.

Of course, in time the wagon was replaced by a proper bus, but that was long after I had graduated and was attending college.

When I entered high school, sixteen units were required for graduation: four in English, four in Latin, four in history, and four in mathematics. There was a single science course without benefit of laboratory work, and later an elective course called Social Problems. No vocational courses were offered for at least six years. The library was a single bookcase in a classroom. No cafeteria and no indoor plumbing existed.

When I left high school for college, I had not been able to spend a complete year of schooling at home during the entire time, with the exception of the year when Aunt Gay taught me at home. I had never attended school at any time with Marguerite. Her efforts to get an education were as fraught with difficulties as mine. During elementary school, she had lived with an aunt and attended a two-room school at Dragonville. At the beginning of her high school work, her mother had rented a house at Stevensville and moved there for the school year with her three children, all of whom were in school. At the end of the session, the family returned to their home.

Recognizing the necessity for securing an education, our parents paid whatever price was required to achieve it. We did not expect or demand that everything come with ease and little effort. Perseverance and determination were lessons learned in many ways on a farm.

CHAPTER VIII

Watching Geneva

"Louise," Aunt Hettie said to me one day, "your sharp eyes don't miss much. Watch Geneva for me tomorrow, and I'll bake you a whole batch of sugar cookies."

The promise of cookies and her flattery worked; furthermore, I was lonesome for Marguerite who had not come home that weekend. She attended school at Dragonville and stayed with Aunt Hettie's sister who was one of the teachers. I felt that the task of watching Geneva would be more interesting than my usual chores. It was almost an adult assignment, and it meant that Aunt Het trusted me.

Geneva was the turkey hen. She and the big gobbler, Herman, named for a neighbor, were important barnyard residents because Aunt Hettie raised turkeys seriously. They were her money crop. In the fall if she had ten or twelve birds to sell, her bank account would show a nice increase.

Turkeys were recently domesticated wild fowls. By nature, they were shy birds which had not taken completely to our civilized ways. For instance, they scorned buildings, preferring to roost in a tree, but they were willing to accept the grain thrown out to farm poultry and ate happily though not greedily with the other fowl. During the day, turkeys scattered, seeking food and ranging as far as a mile or more from the barnyard. As night approached, they came home to roost.

The nesting habits of a turkey hen were a carry-over from her wild state. In early spring she would "steal a nest" as Aunt Het put it, locating it in a spot which met her requirements for seclusion. However, the chance of predators rifling the nest were high, and the survival of poults hatched in the wild was low.

Aunt Het always watched the turkey hen, found the nest, retrieved the eggs, and replaced them with a few china eggs, or some hen eggs. After the clutch was complete, she set the eggs under a domestic hen. When hatching time came, the baby birds received her constant care. These were the days before poultry breeding became a big business, and success in raising turkeys came from careful attention.

For several days Aunt Het had been attempting to keep an eye on Geneva, but the bird had eluded her. Now busy with numerous farm chores, she had turned to me for help.

Realizing the important responsibility entrusted to me, I arrived early Saturday morning while Uncle Richie was scattering a bucket of shelled corn on the ground, and barnyard fowls were gobbling it in companionable confusion. Herman and Geneva were together on the edge of the big, noisy circle of birds. Aunt Het was at the well drawing a bucket of water and instructed me carefully. "Don't get too close, Lousie. If Geneva thinks you are watching her, she'll lead you on a wild goose chase. Never go to the nest. Keep her in sight but pretend you are playing. She's pretty smart, you know."

Remembering my instructions, I kept a discreet distance. I was anticipating a lovely day in the open. It was April, the sun was shining, I had some cookies and an apple, and would have had a book but my mother had made me put it down as I was leaving the house, remarking that I could not read and watch the turkey too. Watching Geneva would be a welcome change, I thought, from dusting and running errands.

As the turkey picked her way busily about the barn lot, I loitered by a big sycamore tree and gathered johnny-jump-ups. Apparently Geneva thought I was no threat and she moved forward. I caught a flash of wings as she sailed over the rail fence and landed in the cow lot. There she moved from one clump of grass to another, inspecting each carefully for bugs or seeds. She scratched busily in a patch of sand looking for gravel. At last satisfied, she stretched out on her side, spread her wings, and sunned herself in a great show of relaxation. "She is not going to lay today," I thought. A turkey did not always lay an egg each day; perhaps today she would indeed "lead me on a wild goose chase." I grew bored. I ate a few cookies, watched some ants carry off a crumb, saw my father harness Mac and Woodrow to plow our garden, and wondered if I hadn't as well go home. I looked around finally and found that Geneva was nowhere in sight!

Chagrined, I climbed the fence and ran across the cow lot, looking everywhere. I was about to give up in tears when she reappeared on the other side of the fence and started across a freshly plowed field making for the woods on the farther side. There was nothing to do but follow. Soon I was lifting heavy, mud-caked feet as I slowly made my way toward the woods. Geneva reached them first, of course, and was immediately lost from view.

I kept my eyes on the place where she had entered, and when I arrived at the spot, peered in all directions but saw and heard nothing. She was gone. I was disappointed, ashamed, tired, and hungry. Hesitating to go home in disgrace, I sat down on the soft needles beneath a pine tree, leaned my head on the trunk, and wept. I must have dozed too, for by now it was past midday. I awoke suddenly to hear a faint rustling of leaves a few yards away. There was Geneva emerging from a little hollow screened by some briars and brush. She had been in plain view all the time, but her protective coloration had been a perfect shield blending with the soft browns and grays of the dry leaves in the hollow. She must have thought I was not worth bothering about and, tiring of trying to evade me, had gone to her nest, laid her egg, and was now ready to return to the business of the day. She had made no sound. A hen cackled in excitement when she had laid an egg, but a turkey did not advertise.

I watched until she had left, crept forward, pulled the briars aside, scratching my hands and face as I did so, and stared at the four large speckled eggs that lay there. Aunt Hettie had been right. It was important to find the nest and save the eggs before foxes got them.

So intent had I been on my discovery that I was not aware of the change in the weather. A hard April shower fell as I came out into the field. I raced toward the house and arrived wet, cold, scratched, muddy, shivering, but triumphant. My sharp eyes had found the nest, and I had proved that I could do a grown-up's job.

Geneva laid fifteen eggs that spring. Aunt Het visited the nest each day, carefully removing the egg of the day and leaving a hen egg in its place so that the number grew daily. Geneva's maternal instincts apparently were not very strong for she abandoned the nest readily after her egg-laying stint ended. Perhaps she was stung by Herman's indifference; he had not visited the nest once during the whole period.

The speckled eggs hatched under Aunt Hettie's watchful eye. She had given them over to a large broody Rhode Island Red hen whose determination to set was evident. After twenty-eight days, as each baby bird, a feeble, weak, little creature, left the shell, Aunt Het removed it from the nest, wrapped it in soft rags and took it to her kitchen where she kept it warm until it could eat. If left in the nest, the baby turkeys were often mashed by the hen and killed.

My interest in this flock of turkeys was proprietary. I was even allowed to feed them the hard-boiled egg, mashed to a fine meal, which was their first food. No specially prepared mash was even available in those days.

The young poults were kept in an enclosure, away from the farm fowls until they were half-grown, before they were allowed to range the barnyard. I often helped to "get them up" that summer when a storm was coming. The young birds seemed to have no idea of self-preservation and often would drown in a heavy downpour. Getting them up was no easy task because turkeys are the most perverse and stupid of birds. They would run around the coop ignoring the opening, fly over it, or take off in the opposite direction. With black clouds piling up and thunder rolling, it was a frustrating, maddening job almost impossible to do alone.

That Aunt Het raised ten turkeys that year was due to her untiring vigilance and constant care, but that year I had a share in her success. I had found the nest.

CHAPTER IX

The Wheat Harvest

A ripening field of wheat is a beautiful sight. In early June it is a pale green sea which glistens in the sunlight and with a slight breeze moves in smooth undulations like the water in a mill pond. As the grain matures, the color changes to gold; the slender wheat stalks supporting the heads of grain turn a deeper gold with each passing day. A breeze stirs the field to motion, the ripples move in patterns like shadows deepening and darkening in one place, glowing and shining in another. When the field is dark gold with the stalks still erect, it is time to cut the wheat. To wait means that the heavy heads bend the stalks, they break, and grain is lost in cutting.

After supper one June evening, my father and I viewed our field taking in its beauty and rejoicing in the prospects of a good crop.

"It will be ready to cut by Tuesday, I think." He sounded pleased. "I'll have to round up some hands to help. Want to ride with me?"

"Of course."

"Go tell Mother and meet me at the barn. We can be back before dark."

I hurried to the kitchen to tell my mother that we would ride up to the colored settlement about a mile away to get help with wheat cutting. My father had harnessed faithful Mac to the road-cart and, taking me between his knees, we set off.

A road cart was a two-wheeled, one-horse vehicle with a single seat. Light in weight, it was fast and, therefore, a favorite with my father. He had a boy's pleasure in speed and loved to drive his horse at a good clip when the roads were dry and good. When I went with him, I sat on the narrow seat between his knees while his feet rested on the shafts. The shafts passed through loops on the harness which were all that held the vehicle and horse together. Once when I was with him, the horse's girth broke, the shafts dropped to the ground, and we both tumbled forward. When we stopped, I was holding gentle Mac's tail while the horse looked over his shoulder at us wondering, no doubt, what was the matter.

Cutting wheat was an important annual event which involved special preparations and extra help. The reaper, or binder as we called it, was a machine for cutting the stalks and binding them into sheaves. Used only once a year, it had to be taken from the shed, examined to be sure it was in working order, then greased and made ready for the field. On the day the wheat was cut, several "hands" followed the machine, and as it dropped bundles of wheat straw, set them upright into small stacks. At the end of the day, the field where waving grain had once stood now looked like an Indian encampment with teepees scattered over the stubble.

If a heavy rain came and wet the sheaves of wheat, the stacks had to be separated, the bundles laid out to dry and restacked later. It was important to keep the grain dry until it could be threshed. Damp grain became moldly and musty and did not make good flour.

The really big day of the farming season, however, was the threshing day. A threshing machine usually served an area of four or five miles. The operator of the machine would move it from farm to farm, threshing each farmer's crop for a percentage of the yield or for a cash price agreed upon with the farmer. Usually, there were several men, experienced in handling the equipment, who worked the operation at each farm, but my father also called on neighbors to help. Uncle Richie would bring his wagon and Mr. Dyke, another neighbor, would do the same. They loaded bundles of grain from the field and brought them to the thresher. When the thresher moved to their places, my father would go with his wagon and return the work.

The thresher usually pulled into our place late in the afternoon and "set down." This meant that a suitable location convenient to my father's barn was selected; the wheels were blocked with logs to prevent movement. The gasoline engine which powered the thresher had to be "set down" also and a belt from the engine connected to the thresher. Every preparation for the next day was made to ensure an early start.

On the morning of the threshing, my mother, Aunt Gay, and I would begin to prepare the mid-day meal for the workmen as soon as breakfast was over. The black Majestic range, still hot from breakfast, would be kept going constantly until dinner was over. Five or six heads of cabbage, a bucket of potatoes, a huge kettle of beets, or whatever vegetables were available in the garden, would be put on to cook. A piece of ham or shoulder, cooked the previous day, would be waiting. A cherry or apple cobbler for dessert was made next; then we would make corn bread pones to be "soaked bread." This strange delicacy was nothing more than bread over which the "liquor" from the cooked cabbage or other greens was poured. Finally four or five dozen biscuits would be mixed, rolled, cut, and baked. Gallons of tea would be ready. When the dinner hour approached, I would be dispatched to the ice house for ice so that the men, hot and dusty from the morning's work, could have the treat of iced tea. Not every farmer had an ice house so a cold drink was a rarity.

There would be five or six white men to eat in the dining room and just as many hands who were served in the kitcen, though the food was identical. Added to the menu would be large dishes of preserves to go with hot biscuits, and, of course, pickle.

The men lined up at the well to wash their dusty faces and hands and then trooped to the house eager for a big meal. By one o'clock the men would be back at work and Mother, Auntie, and I would be faced with a mountain of greasy dishes.

Sometimes I would be pressed into service to tally the wheat. As each bushel measure left the thresher, it was brought to the grain barn to be emptied. I would make a mark for each measure and at the fifth the mark was diagonal (卌). It was easy to count the yield by fives at the end of the day. I was delighted to undertake this task, as it made me feel important to be part of the activity around the barn.

The thresher made a tremendous racket; as wheat was fed into its maw, it separated the grain from chaff (the cover of the individual grains) and straw (the stalks). The chaff was blown out to fall in piles at the back of the machine; the straw came out there also but men with pitchforks moved it as fast as it fell. They carried it a few yards and made great, towering stacks to be used later as bedding for horses and cattle. One stack was always mine to play on. I could climb up its loose sides and slide down bringing straw with me to create an unsightly litter and it was accepted, but I was not to play on the others.

The organization and teamwork that went on at the wheat harvest was tremendous. The men loved the excitement of trying to keep ahead of the wagons waiting to be unloaded; they enjoyed the competition and the joking that went on among the crowd. Hot, noisy, tiring, but exhilarating, wheat threshing was a group effort that made a break in the rather lonely work of plowing and planting. Harvesting a field of wheat today is done quickly and efficiently by combines that cut and thresh the grain in one operation. It lacks the drama and excitement, however, of the old-fashioned method.

Playing on the straw stacks in late evening when the sun was down and fireflies were out was a favorite romp for visiting children. There might be five or six of us. Marguerite and her visiting cousin, Frankie, Billy, Anne, and I and possibly more. We would swarm up the side of my stack and slide down the opposite side in a welter of loose straw, pick ourselves up and, shrieking and screaming, climb up again. We soon had bits of straw in our hair and clothing. The straw looked clean but there was a great deal of dust resulting from our violent running, sliding, and jumping. Perspiring freely, we were soon hot and sticky and dusty but glowing with excitement.

We gave no thought to our discomfort as long as we could see to play. At last, the group separated to go home to chiding parents who cleaned us up and sent us to bed.

When we grew a little older, this game became too tame. Someone had the bright idea that we could jump from the roof of the grain barn onto the pile of straw and add to the fun. There was a persimmon tree growing conveniently by the garden fence, its branches spreading over part of the flat, sloping roof of the grain barn. Like a swarm of monkeys, we climbed the fence, pulled up into the tree, ran across the roof, leaped toward the stack to land on the straw, to slide down and race back to the tree to repeat the performance. All but Anne found it great fun; she never got up nerve enough to try it.

This went on for several days, until a heavy rain revealed some leaks in the barn roof. Mystified, my father could not see why his new tarpaper roof was leaking. By chance, he saw us in our new game one evening and realized that our bare feet were making cracks in the paper. After that we were forbidden to use the barn roof as a launching pad for our jumps.

We soon found another roof, however. This was a wood shingled roof that formed a shed for the cows. When new straw was piled in the cow lot, we could jump from the shed roof and burrow through the loosely piled straw. One afternoon there were six at play. My mother was keeping Ed Wilshin, the young son of a widowed cousin, while she was attending summer school. Ed was resourceful and inventive about games, and he had come up with a new twist.

"Frankie, let's play tag. See who can climb up the roof and jump before he's tagged."

"That's not hard. Bet you can't tag me," called Billy who promptly scrambled up the fence, onto the roof, and over into the straw.

"Bet, I can," yelled Ed and was after him in a second.

"Watch me, Ed," I called. "You can't catch me," and I started up behind him. The game was fun with the new element of competition. Beside the fence were several stobs; they had been driven around a length of log to hold it in place, but for some reason, the log had been removed. The stakes were ten or twelve inches high and were a real hazard if someone fell on them. We had not noticed them in our eagerness to climb the fence and reach the roof, but as the game got faster we were becoming more and more excited and careless. Poor Anne stood there in envy and fear as we squealed with delight when someone was tagged or made it to safety. Both were equally exciting.

Finally Ed, in a burst of speed to avoid being tagged by Billy, who was close behind him, lost his footing, slipped and fell to the ground among the stobs. Strangely enough, he curled himself in and around them escaping serious injury except for a scrape on his arm. We gathered around him in fright.

"Gosh, Ed, you could have been killed," said Marguerite. "Suppose you'd hit your stomach on one of those sticks or your eye!" She paled at the thought. Anne was in tears.

"I knew somebody would get hurt. You ought to stop. Please stop," she begged.

Sobered, we ended our frolic for the night. Somehow, playing in the straw never seemed as much fun after that.

Soon after wheat threshing, my mother would ask my father, "When are you going to the mill?"

"I'll send Connie next week if we get a good day. Some new flour would be good."

Our flour was made from the wheat grown on the farm and the supply was apt to be nearly out by the time of the new harvest.

The mill was located on a millpond about fifteen miles away. Essex Mill ground wonderful flour and was patronized by residents of both Essex and King and Queen Counties. The mill was operated by a wheel which turned as water from the pond, conducted through a spillway, rushed into the huge troughs located along its rim. Made of oak and standing twelve feet or more in diameter, the wheel drove the heavy upper millstone, causing it to rotate slowly against the nether stone. These stones were grooved and roughened to form the grinding surface. Grain, such as wheat, passed between the stones which ground it to a fine powder. The flour was then transported by elevators to an upper floor where it was sieved to produce three grades: flour, seconds, and grudgings, a course mixture containing the husks of the wheat.

The building which housed the machinery of a mill was usually three stories high, the height being necessary to provide space for the elevators which lifted the ground flour to sieves on the upper floors.

I seldom went to mill and only when my father was making the trip. It was a long day for a child. The wagon loaded with ten or fifteen bushels of wheat would leave early in the morning and would not reach the mill in under three hours. While the wheat was being ground, the driver and wagon waited to take the flour home. The millpond was a quiet beautiful spot, cool and inviting. The sound of the water pouring over the spillway was drowned by the roar of the machinery when it was in operation, but pleasant to hear when the mill was quiet. Inside everything was a misty white from the fine coating of flour that settled on the floors, cobwebs in the corners, bags of grain, buckets and measures, and even the bushy eyebrows of the miller.

The miller exacted a toll of the wheat for grinding. When the work was finished, the wagon made its slow way home. That night my mother would try the new flour with a batch of feather-light biscuits, and my father would smile contentedly.

A good wheat harvest was very important to the economy of our family.

CHAPTER X

Travel

In the first decades of the twentieth century travel was slow and difficult for people who did not live near steamboat or rail lines. It is possible to go from New York to San Francisco in less time today than it took to go from my home to Richmond in 1915. For the owner of a car, the time could be reduced somewhat, but the lack of bridges over rivers and the poor roads still made the difficulties stupendous.

I remember two trips which I took before I was eight years old, and they were major events. The first was a visit to Irvington, a small town on the North shore of the Rappahannock River, and the second was a trip to Richmond.

Cousin Gay Wilshin had invited Mother and me to visit her in Irvington, so leaving Aunt Gay to keep house and look after my father, we embarked on my first ride on a steamboat. My father drove us in the buggy to Bowler's Wharf to take the boat. The *Middlesex,* considered one of the handsomest boats on the Rappahannock, made regular runs to Fredericksburg. On the return trip she stopped at wharves on both sides of the river, taking on passengers and freight bound for Baltimore.

We arrived at the wharf about an hour before the steamer was due. Passengers had to walk the long pier to the deepwater landing where the vessel could dock. The shallow shore extended out a great distance; the pier was said to be a mile in length. As we hurried along, a deafening blast from the ship's horn announced her approach, the sound echoing from shore to shore.

"There's the boat, Daddy. Look, here it comes! Oh, isn't it beautiful," I cried in wild excitement.

"Hush, Baby. It is not ladylike to make so much noise," admonished my mother.

The *Middlesex* drew near enough for me to see the coiling smoke belching from the great black smoke stack amid ships. As it came nearer, I watched the prow split the water making a curtain of white foam along its sides. Several flags were flying, but I recognized only one, the flag of the United States on its stern. As it approached the wharf, I could see a crowd of passengers at the rail and deck hands running about. A bell began to ring as the captain reversed the engines, and the steamer pulled in the wharf. The gangplank was quickly lowered and fashionably dressed men and women began to walk down it to be greeted by others in the crowd waiting on the pier.

"We'll go aboard as soon as all the passengers are off," said my father as I tugged impatiently at his hand.

Just then I noted the deck hands prodding two calves toward the gangplank.

"Stop twisting that calf's tail," I shouted stung to fury by the sight. "You're hurting it. Stop it."

Mother put her hand over my mouth, and my father picked me up, holding me with one arm and our suitcase with the other.

"Let's get aboard," he said. "Be quiet, Louise. They do that to get the calves on the boat. They'll stop soon."

All around us was bedlam. Deckhands were carrying baskets of potatoes, tomatoes, and beans aboard. Crates of chickens were waiting to be loaded. One man was pushing toward the gangplank a hand truck with a steer in a large crate. People were shouting, calves were bleating mournfully, and hens were cackling. I was beside myself at the rough treatment the poor animals were receiving.

"Why are they putting them on the boat? Where are they going?" I begged.

"These things are produce being shipped to commission merchants in Baltimore. Remember when I shipped old Boris last fall. That's where he went," answered my father.

"I don't like it. I wish you'd make them stop hurting the animals." I was ready to cry.

We pushed forward until we were in the central dining room where there were seats around the wall as well as at the tables. We did not come back on deck until we heard the purser call:

"All ashore that's going ashore," and my father hurried to leave before the boat departed.

Mother and I sat on the deck for most of the trip. We did not have a stateroom because we reached our destination that afternoon. When we left the steamboat about four o'clock, we had been on the way from home since 8:00 a.m. It had taken almost all day to travel some twenty miles.

Cousin Gay's home stood on a little creek. I thought it strange to look out the bedroom window and see water and a rowboat tied to a dock a few yards from the house. She told us her two sons rowed across the creek to go to school. Ed and Francis were active youngsters who dived from the dock and swam in the creek while I watched with envy and amazement.

Our visit lasted several days; then we caught the boat on her up-river swing and returned to Bowlers, where my father met us for the eight mile trip back home.

Exciting as this experience was, it was nothing compared to our trip to Richmond. This was true for several reasons. First, the trip was much more complicated to accomplish, and the city was much more amazing to see, but added to these, I had my first picture taken by a real photographer!

Arrangements for the visit had to be made well in advance with Cousin Irene. Mother wrote asking if it would be convenient for us to spend the week of September 16-23 with her and, if so, would she arrange for a portrait sitting for me. Her reply came in several days and we began to make ready. Mother made a new dress for herself and started a very fancy one for me for the picture. I, of course, told Marguerite about the proposed trip "and I'm going to have my picture made" I ended triumphantly.

"That's nothing, Don't brag about it. Sister had hers done last year. It didn't hurt." Marguerite was unimpressed.

I was somewhat squelched, but I did not give up.

"Cousin Irene says he's the best photographer in Richmond. Where did Sister have hers made? I want to see it."

"Come on; I'll race you to the ice house." Marguerite ignored my question and was off like a flash.

A day or two later, when we were playing at her house, she eyed me seriously and came forth with a startling announcement.

"Your hair needs cutting. It's hanging down around your ears. If it was cut off, Aunt Kate wouldn't have to roll it up every night and you'd look better. I'll cut it for you."

It sounded like a fine idea to me. It was true, as my mother often said, "If Marguerite told Louise to stick her head in the fire, she'd do it." I seldom questioned her judgment. After all, she was two and a half years older than I and knew everything.

We went to Aunt Het's bedroom and found her dress-making scissors to use.

"Sit here by the stove and hold still or I might cut your ear." Marguerite held the shears threateningly. She took up a lock of my fine blond hair in her left hand and snipped it off without hesitation. Snip. Snip. She caught up another clump, cut it, and dropped it into the stove where it fell on last winter's ashes.

Snip. Snip. In deep absorption she continued across the back while I sat still as a mouse. At last she came to stand in front of me. Her blue eyes squinted as she surveyed her handiwork.

"Needs more off the front." Snip. Snip.

At last it was done. I ran my hand around the back of my neck and began to tremble.

"Does it look better? Really?" I was uncertain by then.

"Of course it does, you goose." Marguerite tossed her own curls to prove it.

Just then Aunt Het called us to the dinner table where Uncle Richie was waiting for us to take our places before saying grace.

"Will you have ham, Louise?" he asked, grace over, and looked at me fully for the first time.

"Punkin, when did you cut your hair?" he asked using his pet name for me.

"Just now. Marguerite cut it for me. It's cooler." I was pleased at his having noticed.

"Yes, I'm sure it is," he answered and glanced at Aunt Het with a strange look. She rolled her eyes heavenward and passed the biscuits.

After dinner Marguerite and I sought the cool of the spring and began to hunt for crayfish.

"Louise, Louise." Mother's voice penetrated the thick shade under the sycamore.

"Mother is calling. Come on and go with me," I invited, but Marguerite shook her head.

"I've got to catch this old crayfish before he gets away. You go on."

"Yes Ma'm, I'm coming," I yelled and ran for the stile over the fence that separated our two properties.

Mother looked up from her sewing and smiled.

"I want you to try on your new dress before I hem it. It has to be finished today because we leave tomorrow." Mother had not even glanced at me until then; now she pulled her glasses up on the top of her head and gazed at me, a look of consternation creeping over her face.

"What on earth has happened to you?" For a split second she hesitated, then burst into tears. "Sister, come here and look at Louise. Lord, have mercy," she sobbed.

Auntie came running. Ordinarily she took my side, but she too became angry.

"Who did this? You! Surely you have some sense— and your mother making you a beautiful dress for your picture. Louise, you ought to be spanked. I'm ashamed of you." Her words hurt like bee stings.

"Marguerite did it," I burst out. "She said it would look better, and Mother wouldn't have to curl it, and it's cooler."

"Marguerite should be whipped. She knows better than this; she's two years older, but I know Hettie won't touch her. I'll just go and tell Brother Richie about this." Aunt Gay's temper was up.

"No, Sister. Don't do that. It will just cause trouble," said Mother who was always the peacemaker.

When my father came for supper, the tale was repeated. Two angry women and a miserable child confronted him. What to do? We couldn't call off the trip; there was no way to let all the people involved know that we would not come. The nearest telephone, so necessary to modern communication, was at least twenty miles away.

"You'll have to go on, Kate," said my father. "You can decide about the picture after you get to Irene's, but it is a shame." He too was disapproving and disappointed in me.

In great distress now, I hurried into the yard and climbed the maple tree, my favorite refuge when things were bad. Its leafy branches hid me, and I could cry without being seen. I thought over the episode and a strange doubt of Marguerite's motives began to take shape in my childish mind. As I often did, I came up with a rhyme:

> My hair is gone
> And I look bad.
> Marguerite did it
> And she is glad. Amen.

I felt better as I decided to get even someday for this ugly trick. It was several months, however, before the opportunity came.

Our journey began the next morning when we left home at 3:30 a.m. to drive to Water Fence, a crossing on the Mattaponi River about fifteen miles away. It was pitch dark as we set out. A few stars were shining, but we carried a lantern until daybreak. As the first streaks of light appeared, I began to rouse from the doze of the first eight or ten miles. The twitter of awakening birds in the trees, the steady plop-plop of Mac's hooves, and the little tuneful whistle that my father entertained himself with on long drives, brought me back to reality.

"Where are we?" I yawned and looked around.

"Passing Mt. Olive Church," Daddy answered. "Go back to sleep. It's a long way yet."

I twisted into a new position and slept again.

"Whoa, Mac. Wake up, Baby. Here we are."

It was daylight now with the rim of sun showing red above the horizon. We were standing before a river and a man was coming from a house to the right.

"Good morning, Capt. Spencer. Can you take us across the river? My wife is catching the train to Richmond this morning. You got my letter to expect us, I hope." My father was all business.

"Yes, Mr. Eubank. I'll be ready in a minute. Tie your horse and put your things in the boat," he answered.

I stared at the little rowboat tied to the piling of the dock. After the mighty *Middlesex,* this craft seemed pitifully small to trust ourselves to, but Mother was getting out of the buggy being careful that her long skirts did not brush against the wheel. I settled my tam o'shanter on my head hoping that it hid my notched hair and followed her to the dock.

Capt. Spencer jumped into the boat steadying it as my father helped Mother, then handed me over to the boatmen. Last, he followed us in. The captain untied the boat, took up the oars, and began to pull for the opposite shore. The river was narrow at that point and the crossing took only about fifteen minutes. As the bottom of the boat grated on the sand of the shore, he called out:

"Mr. Brooks! Oh, Mr. Brooks. Here's your fare."

A sandy-haired man in a wide brimmed hat approached. A horse and buggy were standing near the landing.

"Morning, Cap'n. Right on time, are ye? And this is Mr. and Mrs. Eubank, ain't it?" He bowed to Mother and shook hands with my father. "We better hurry. Train's due at 7:30 a.m., and its 7:00 now."

"Have a good trip, Mother. I'll meet you next Thursday. Goodbye, Baby. I'll miss you helping with the chickens." Daddy hugged us both, helped us into Mr. Brooks' buggy, then returned to the boat where Capt. Spencer was waiting to row back across the river.

We had two miles to drive to Romancoke, the little station in the woods where the train stopped for passengers.

"Hope my watch ain't wrong," said the man as we reached the lonely little building. He got out, laid his ear to the rail and listened. "She's coming, ma'm," he said to Mother. "I hear her 'bout a mile away, I reckon. Come on while I run this flag up." He took our bags and stepped quickly to the station to raise a wooden arm with a red flag on it.

We waited with mounting excitement as we heard the rumble on the tracks and then the plaintive whistle as the train came into view and began to slow for the stop. Mother paid Mr. Brooks and reminded him of our return. "We'll be on the train next Thursday. Please meet us to take us back to the river. Be here without fail."

"Yes ma'm. You can depend on it. I'll be here," he said as he handed our bag to the conductor, and we climbed into the train.

The thing had looked like a monster to me as it came roaring into view. The sound of the escaping steam, the whistle, and the grating rumble of the wheels on the tracks were both frightening and exhilarating. I climbed the steps with my heart pounding. I was really going to ride on a train! The coach was long and narrow with rows of high-backed seats, covered in red plush, on each side of the aisle. We sat down while the conductor took our money. Immediately the whole thing began to move, trees flew by the windows, and the conductor swayed as he walked the aisle. Suddenly the mournful whistle sounded again. Mother seemed unconcerned, but I could not take my eyes from the exciting surroundings. I watched the scene flashing by, then back to shiny brass handles on the seats, the lovely red upholstery, and the many people riding with us. It seemed to me that we were traveling at an incredible speed as indeed we were, compared to a horse-drawn vehicle.

We arrived in Richmond at 11:05 o'clock to find Cousin Irene waiting for us. The Main Street Station in Richmond, for many years the only one in the city, was breathtaking in its size and elegance. Overawed, I stumbled along after Mother gazing at the red-caps (porters), the hurrying crowds, and the vaulted ceiling of the station. Leaving the station, we went out into the street, where new wonders awaited us.

I had never seen buildings so big, so close together and so many people going in all directions. We stopped at the corner and waited until the street car came along. After the train, this seemed less impressive, but fascinating, as it moved slowly through the streets taking on and discharging passengers. We passed enormous churches, many stores, and a pretty park with a summerhouse in the center. How exciting, how different from the farm! But it was no place to live I decided.

When we arrived at Cousin Irene's home, Billy and Anne greeted us with delight and were eager to show me the wonders of their way of life. I saw my first bathroom. Water came out of the pipes when I turned a little handle. There was an immense white bathtub with claw feet, and a flush toilet, the greatest marvel of all. When it began to grow dark, Cousin Irene turned on the gas and lighted it. This seemed almost magic to me—no lamps to fill with oil, no chimneys to clean, but a bright, steady, blue flame that lighted the entire room.

That night, I slept fitfully, wakened by the clatter of the street car every time it passed and puzzled by the room which never became dark because of the street lights. Each time I was aroused, I thrilled again to think that I was really in the city.

Next morning after breakfast the subject of the picture to be made came up.

"Irene, what shall I do about Louise's picture? Look at her hair. Marguerite took matters into her own hands and cut it. It looks simply terrible." Mother was still upset by my appearance and so was I.

"It is a shame." responded Cousin Irene, "but if you have the picture taken full face and put a big bow in her hair, maybe it won't look too bad."

On Monday we kept the appointment. My mother dressed me carefully in the new frock, fussed over my few strands of hair, placed the blue bow strategically on the left side, and mourned constantly over Marguerite's perfidy.

"That child should be punished. She was bound to know she was ruining your looks. The picture can't do you justice. I could shake that little vixen."

Posing me in various positions, the photographer worked in vain to get a smile. Near tears, I was humiliated and ashamed. My idol Marguerite had turned on me, I thought; everyone was laughing at me, and, worst of all, the picture would record the episode permanently. The picture today shows a glum, miserable child in spite of the pretty dress.

When my father saw the picture, he shook his head. "Why didn't you smile, Baby? You'd be my own pretty little girl then. I hardly know this solemn little statue."

I couldn't speak. Pretty! He'd said PRETTY, but everybody knew I was ugly. I resolved then and there to smile as much as possible, if that's what it took to be pretty.

A great believer in prayer, I often prayed that God would make me pretty and, when a quick trip to the mirror revealed no change, I was deeply disappointed.

Our trip to Richmond ended with our return on Thursday. Reversing the process, we left the station at 7:30 a.m., arrived in Romancoke at noon, and made our

way home by way of Mr. Brooks' buggy, Capt. Spencer's
boat, and my father's faithful Mac and our buggy after we
had crossed the river. It was dark when we returned.

Such slow and difficult travel meant that trips
assumed gigantic importance and were not attempted
very often.

The author at age 5

CHAPTER XI

The Ice House

Lack of refrigeration was a serious problem for everyone, from the days of the early settlers until the advent of manufactured ice. People in our area attempted to solve the problem in various ways. Some built "milk houses" in which cool water from the well was piped into deep, zinc-lined trays in which they placed pans of milk and bowls of butter. Some put coolers in the spring over night to keep butter firm or milk from turning sour; others used the well, hanging a bucket into its cool depths by a rope. More well-to-do families built an ice house which provided ice for the table, but still the waste in food was enormous.

In extremely hot weather, very little food could be carried over from one day to the next. Biscuits turned moldy, milk and vegetables soured, fresh meat spoiled, butter became rancid, and fresh fruit rotted quickly. Eggs, which were usually fertile, would go bad quickly and make a horrible smell. Salt pork was a standby in all homes, probably because, preserved by the salt, it could be kept for longer periods of time. To keep cream sweet enough to make good butter in mid-summer, my mother resorted to skimming the cream from the milk and lowering it into the well until churning time. As it was, left over food was fed to the hogs, but it kept someone in the hot kitchen preparing three meals a day. When the weather turned cool in the fall, we kept food easily on the back porch in a pie safe (a cupboard with perforated tin panels); in winter it became a real refrigerator except that care had to be taken not to have bowls and pitchers broken when the contents froze.

We were grateful to have an ice house. There had been one on the property since my grandfather's day, but the one I remember had been built by my father and Uncle Richie at a convenient location for use by both families.

It was built on the pattern of the earlier one, thirty feet deep with a six-foot well in the center for drainage. It was lined on all four sides with logs placed vertically from the bottoms to ground level. The sides sloped outward so that it was wider at the top. The bottom, as I recall, was covered with a floor of logs laid side by side, and a second layer laid in the opposite direction. This kept them in place and allowed water from the melting ice to drain into the center well. On this floor were piled several feet of wheat straw, pine needles, or sawdust. The ice pit was covered with a low slab roof which almost touched the ground. A door in front opened to the dark interior.

Ice was harvested in winter when a period of prolonged cold produced ice three or four inches thick. Our ice pond was made by damming a stream and flooding a low area. It was not very deep. When the ice was thick enough, Uncle Richie and my father would each harness his team to a wagon and go to the pond to cut ice. Wearing heavy boots and thick socks, they waded into the water, cut blocks of ice with an axe, and pushed them to shore. They loaded the ice on their wagons, drove to the pit, and dumped it in. Layers of straw, or other insulating material, were put between the huge blocks. Sometimes it required several freezes to harvest enough to fill the house. It was a long, cold, disagreeable job, which the men did cheerfully, looking forward to cooling drinks on hot summer days.

In hot weather, as meal time approached, I would be sent to the ice house to get the ice for dinner. Sometimes Marguerite, on a similar errand, would meet me there. We would dig through the thick straw until we found a block of ice, chip off some pieces, and run home with it before it melted. As the season advanced, the level in the ice house fell so that, by late summer, it was necessary to descend a ladder to reach the ice.

One day with a house full of company, Mother dispatched me with a large bucket and an ice pick to get the ice.

"Hurry, Baby, everything is ready and your father will be here in a minute," she said.

I ran off willingly enough, descended the ladder in the gloom, found the pitchfork, removed enough straw to reach a big block, filled my bucket, replaced the straw, and was ready to return when I saw a huge black snake between me and the ladder. Trapped, I cowered in the corner afraid to take my eyes off the snake which kept its beady eyes fixed on me. Occasionally it opened its mouth and ran out its forked tongue. I was petrified. Time passed. I could hear faint calls for me from the direction of the house, but I was afraid to answer.

Daddy will come soon. When I don't come back, he'll come to look for me, I told myself. Resolutely I waited; it seemed an hour, but could have been no more than ten minutes, when a shaft of light fell across the darkness. The door had opened. I could see my father's head in the opening.

"Louise, are you all right? What's the matter?" he called.

Still afraid to move, I answered, "Snake!"

As he started down the ladder, the snake slithered away in the dark corner to the left and out of sight.

"Oh, Daddy, I'm so glad you came. I was scared to death," I began to cry as he picked up the bucket and put his arm around me.

"Black snakes are perfectly harmless. He was just as afraid of you as you were of him. He's gone now. Come on. We're waiting dinner," he replied.

"He's still in the ice house. He can't get out. How could he? I'll never go back there," I quavered as we crossed the field to the house.

"If a snake can climb a tree, he can get out of there, certainly," he reassured me. "You'll never see him again."

After some delay, the ice reached the table, and dinner proceeded. I was the center of attention for a few minutes, the company, Mother, and Auntie sympathizing, and my father looking amused.

One of our summer delights was ice cream. When we had a number of visitors, this proved an entertaining activity.

"Kate, how about some ice cream today. If you'll make the custard, we'll freeze it," Cousin Will or Carl or some male guest would be likely to inquire.

"All right. What kind do you want?" My mother would reply.

"How about caramel? Everybody likes that," would come the answer.

Then Will, or whoever, would set off toward the ice house. Mother would get the eggs and milk for the custard, and prepare to make the caramel syrup. Caramelizing meant putting dry sugar into a heavy iron frying pan over high heat until it melted and burnt a little turning from a clear syrup to a light brown color. To this, she would add cold water and stir, until she had a delicious syrup to add to the custard. This was put into a two gallon metal cylinder which fitted into a wooden bucket which held the crushed ice. By this time the men would have gathered under the walnut tree with a grass bag of ice, and with an axe they would have it crushed and ready to·fill the space between the cylinder and the bucket. When the cylinder was in place inside the freezer, the space between was filled with crushed ice, and coarse salt was poured over it. A top fitted over the cylinder with a long handle which turned cogs causing the inner bucket to turn in the icy brine. The contents were stirred by paddles as the crank was turned briskly. Willing workers eagerly took turns at the crank because when the custard was partly frozen and turning became difficult, the "dasher" or paddles were removed, and those who had helped in the freezing were privileged to taste the custard clinging to the blades. There was competition at the crank for this reason.

"Aren't you tired yet, Will? Let me take a turn," one would say.

"Get out of the way and let a strong man show you how to do it," from another.

"Gosh, it's getting hard to turn. It's almost frozen."

"Come on, Kate. Bring something to put the dasher on and plenty of spoons," someone would call at last as the group under the walnut tree saw their labors reaching the climax.

"It's not ready yet. I haven't put in the cream," my mother would answer and she would come with a quart of rich cream. The freezer would be opened, the cream added, and turning would continue until at last the custard was so stiff that the crank would not turn. This time when the freezer was opened, the dasher would be lifted from the stiff custard and placed on a platter for all to sample.

"Couldn't be better." "Just right." "Don't be a pig; you've got more than your share," and similar banter went on around the freezer. The ladies fanning on the front porch might join the group for more joking, but the delicacy was not to be served until after dinner. The next step was to pour off the brine, plug the hole in the side of the freezer, add more ice and salt, and pack it to finish freezing. Heavily swathed to keep the contents cold, the freezer stood alone and untended under the tree until serving time. The fun of freezing the cream had occupied the morning; the joy of eating it came later after a big dinner. Portions were generous and appetites appeared undiminished when serving time finally came.

Although modern refrigeration is one of the most important technological advances of the twentieth century, the passing of ice harvesting and the ice house closed a colorful part of rural life.

CHAPTER XII

Cleaning The Well

"John, you'll have to have the well cleaned out this morning," my mother announced as my father entered the kitchen.

"What's the matter?" He set the two buckets of fresh milk on the table and looked at her in alarm.

"We can't use the water. It smells terrible. I had to send Connie to Brother Rich's for a bucket before I could cook breakfast, so it will be late. You'll have to do something this morning."

The trouble could not have come at a worse time. It was Saturday and the hands expected half a day off. No one in his right mind worked on Sunday except in an extreme emergency, and though lack of water could certainly be classified as such, my father was the last one to have work done on Sunday. He observed the Biblical law permitting removal of "an ox in the ditch," but inanimate things could wait. However, we had the usual houseful of company (my uncle, his wife, and two small sons), and we could hardly be expected to bring water for all our needs from the next farm for very long. My father did not argue.

"I'll send Connie for Irving Mann now. He can eat breakfast when he gets back," he stated.

"No, I can feed Connie now. Let him hitch the wagon while I get it ready," Mother answered.

Irving Mann was the local well cleaner and husband of Jenny Bell, who helped us occasionally with house cleaning. Irving disdained field work; he reserved his talents for his specialized job and, since cleaning a well occurred seldom, he was usually loafing at home to Jenny Bell's disgust.

"He trifling. Irbing just plain trifling. He don't like work," she would grumble; nevertheless she took pride in the fact that he was able to do a job few other men would tackle.

Uncle Wellie and Aunt Jessie with their small sons, Rodman and Thomas, entered the kitchen in time to learn of the disaster to the well and the trip to find Irving. The boys immediately wanted to ride in the wagon with Connie and this was hastily arranged.

When we finally sat down to breakfast, we heard the creak of the wagon as Connie and the boys departed to fetch Irving and his gear from his home about a mile away.

Our well, dug in 1852 when the house was being built, was over 50 feet deep and yielded a steady flow of soft, sweet water undiminished even in the driest years. Visitors often commented on the flavor of the water which had a low mineral content making it sweet and refreshing as well as soft for laundry purposes.

Water had been drawn for many years by the bucket with ropes passing over a pulley which hung suspended from a frame over the open well. However by 1915, the well had been covered by a neat wellhouse, and a wooden pump had been installed. The first labor-saving device which we acquired, the pump was considered an indication of our progressive thinking.

The wellhouse had a four-sided roof supported by posts, the corners embellished with triangular lattice work. The top was a heavy deck made of six-inch oak boards with a narrow wooden strip nailed over the cracks to keep out trash and rain water.

The wellhouse provided a kind of social center for the farm. Neighbors coming by to borrow the hay balance or a post hole digger would sit on the well deck for a visit before departing. Extra hands called in for field work gathered at the well to await instructions. At the noon hour, men returning from work stopped for long draughts of water and a quick washup before the midday meal. A tin dipper and an enameled wash pan each hung from a nail in the wellhouse. It also provided cover from a sudden shower for men who were caught before they could reach the barn. Visiting children found pumping water fun for a while, and the big barrel positioned under the spout of the pump to catch the run off was, in my opinion, a perfect repository for my captured frogs.

Care had been taken to close the sides of the well top so that nothing could get in. However, small rodents sometimes burrowed through the earth or frogs got into it. The only way to correct this problem was to draw off the water, find the decomposing object, remove it, scrape the well clean, and allow it to refill.

While we waited for the wagon to return, my father and Uncle Wellie pumped water to fill the horse trough and give the stock a supply for the day. In an hour, we heard the wagon approaching, and we all gathered at the well to meet it. The boys were riding proudly by Connie and helping to drive the horses. On the back sat Uncle Combs, who had seen an irresistible opportunity for a ride to and from the farm, and Irving, the man of the hour, with his equipment: a windlass, coils of heavy rope, four sharpened posts, and a huge tub, half a hogshead with holes bored on each side from which hung a tangle of more rope.

Irving began to superintend the removal of his gear and to direct how it was to be set up.

"Keerful wid dat windlass. Don't drap dat tub and tangle dem ropes. Drive them postes in a groun' 'rit chere. Lemme do it, Connie. You don' kno' nuttin' 'bout it."

The men gave him respectful attention recognizing his expertise at well-cleaning, even though they knew he could not plow a straight furrow.

"Louise, run over to Uncle Rich's barn and tell him that we won't be able to overhaul the reaper until later. If he can help here for a while, I'd appreciate it," my father instructed me, and I set off followed to my chagrin, by my shadows, Rodman and Thomas.

When we returned, the men had ripped up the well deck and lifted out the pump, which lay in two sections in the front yard. It looked a bit like a gigantic long-legged crane, its beak the handle, and the two sections of pipe its legs. The dark interior of the well lay exposed. Now they began to position the homemade windlass across the opening. Made of a length of a poplar tree about six inches in diameter, the contraption was crude but efficient. The two posts, driven into the ground at an angle on each side of the well, crossed to form a V and were lashed together to keep them in position. The poplar beam rested on these supports to cross the well, dead center. A handle was fixed securely into each end of the beam to form a crank for turning the machinery. It required a man on each side to operate the windlass as the heavy rope tied in the center was paid out or rewound.

The crucial part involved lowering Irving in his tub to the bottom of the well. The diminutive man, stooped and graying, weighed scarcely 100 pounds. Dressed in hip boots and wearing a ragged stocking cap on his close-cropped hair, he inspected the knots on the ropes attached to the tub and tightened them carefully. He placed a 10-quart bucket to be used for bailing into the tub and pushed it over the well-shaft to swing free while the men at the windlass held it steady.

"Lower away, boys. Take yer time. Steady," he called as he shifted his weight to balance the tub on its long descent. Slowly he disappeared into the abyss.

The crowd around the well pressed toward the opening; the children, fascinated, crept closer to warning cries: "Stop." "Stand back." "Watch out." "Keep out of the way" and "Come here this instant" from Aunt Jessie who captured her boys and held them tightly by the hand as the drama continued.

"Whoa." A faint shout reached the men at the cranks, and they knew that Irving was at the water level. A narrow brick curbing ran around the well just above the water. On this the man stood with a foot on each side as he began to bail water into the tub.

A seemingly long wait followed. At last a jerk on the rope signalled the men at the cranks to bring up the tub. Slowly and carefully the heavy load was raised to the top where it was pulled to the side, and the water was poured on the grass. Empty, it was lowered to where Irving, working in semi-darkness, dipped his bucket into the water to fill the tub again, and the men held the windlass steady. The job required concentration and control on the part of the men working above ground as well as of the solitary worker at the bottom of the well.

The waits became tiresome. The boys lost interest and ran off to play with Pinky and her kittens. The men amused themselve with jokes and conversation. Uncle Combs had been a silent onlooker absorbed in the activities of the day. Perhaps reminded by the stream of water pouring across the yard and down a slope into the roadbed, he raised a question that evidently he had been puzzling over for some time.

"Mis' Shubank," he began watching my father narrowly, "I hear 'em say the yearth turns ober. You don't b'lieve no sech foolishness as dat, do ya?"

Startled by the unexpectedness of the question, my father hesitated a second trying to phrase an answer in terms the old man could understand.

"Why, yes, Uncle Combs, the earth turns ...," he began but was cut off.

"Can't be, man. Why 'twould dreen all the water out de Rappahannock Ribber," his questioner replied in derision. He seemed annoyed that a man whom he respected would subscribe to such absurdity. Before an explanation could be offered, a jerk of the rope called the men at the windlass into action. I watched each tub as it appeared, expecting to see the dead body of some creature in it. More than an hour went by as the tub was raised, emptied, and lowered repeatedly. The small boys, tired of the kittens, found the pool of water in the road more inviting. They soon were muddy from head to toe, their mother unaware of their new activity.

"Irving, how much water is left now?" My father leaned over the edge of the opening and shouted as midday approached. Irving's response was to send up a half-filled tub of water in which floated the decomposing body of a frog. When the tub went down again, almost no water was sent back, but some broken pieces of brick were in the tub. The cause of the trouble having been removed, the well would now be allowed to fill itself.

On the next hoist Irving appeared, wet from head to toe, but grinning, conscious of having successfully completed his job.

"How's the curbing at the bottom look? See any broken places?" my father inquired.

"Yessuh, dey's two-tree places where de bricks is broke off. I g'wine hafta fix it for it for you fo' long," he replied. "She good and tight eber where but dem few places."

"How do you suppose that frog got in there? The cover and sides of the well are tight."

"Lord'a mussy, don' nobody know. Dem things gits anywhere. 'Tis all right now do'. I clean hit out good," Irving stated, basking in the crowd's admiration of his courage and skill.

The windlass was removed, the rope recoiled, the tub drained, and all the gear returned to the wagon as Irving prepared for the trip home. The pump was reassembled and put back, and the cover on top of the well nailed in place. The drama of the morning was over and, except for the pools of water in the yard and the muddy children playing in the road, no one would know of the busy morning we had had.

Connie put the horses back to the wagon, Irving pocketed $2.00, a huge sum for a half day's work, but justified because of its specialized nature and the equipment which he had furnished. He and Uncle Combs climbed back in the wagon, and as it pulled into the road, the boys joined it for their second ride of the day.

"You can't pump any water before tomorrow," my father admonished the crowd at the dinner table. "It will take time for the well to fill again and settle, but the water is perfectly good and ready to use. Irving did a good job, don't you think so, Wellie?"

"Yes, he did," my uncle replied. "I'll tell you one thing. I didn't want to change places with him, did you?"

My father laughed and shook his head.

CHAPTER XIII

Sayings

As a child, I enjoyed the conversation of my elders. I learned what was going on in the family, the church, and the community simply by listening. There were times, however, when the talk was cut off abruptly with the remark:

"Little pitchers have big ears." Mystified at first, I finally understood that I was the "little pitcher" avidly listening to information judged by the adults as unsuitable for one of my age. I bitterly resented being shut out in this fashion. I was not an eavesdropper, but I wanted to know what was going on.

Adult conversation in that day was plentifully larded with aphorisms which had been in use for generations. These sayings required interpretation, but once understood, they made communication easier between young or old. I was brought up on such expressions as the following:

"Pretty is as pretty does."

"Beauty is skin deep, but ugly is to the bone."

"Waste not, want not."

"See a pin and pick it up, all the day you'll have good luck."

"A stitch in time saves nine."

"A new broom sweeps clean."

There are many more which stress thrift or some other virtue.

My mother also had a large store of superstitions which governed her behavior to a remarkable degree. Probably gleaned from her colored nurse, Mammy Fenton, whom she quoted frequently, these ideas had little significance for anyone else. It was bad luck to sweep the dirt out of the door after dark; therefore, if we tidied the kitchen after supper, the little accumulation of trash was left neatly piled by the door until morning. It was also bad luck to have three lighted lamps burning in the same room; thus, we had to make do with two. A garment cut out on Friday had to be finished that day or the owner would not live to wear it out. Many nights I have seen her working until midnight to complete a dress for me that she had begun that morning. It was also bad luck to change a garment if it happened to be put on wrong side out. Wear it like it was rather than run the risk of ill luck.

Descriptions, likewise, were filled with comparisons drawn from rural life which may be almost meaningless today. For instance, our speech has been enriched by many expressions dealing with the domestic hen. "Mad as a wet hen," "fussy as a setting hen," "busy as a hen with one chicken," "running around like a chicken with its head cut off," "cackling like a hen that's just laid an egg," all, to us, evoked a vivid mental picture and conveyed the idea intended. The same was true of the rooster. At one time clocks were owned only by the well-to-do. The rooster performed a needed service when he crowed at day break to announce the beginning of a new day for those who had no way of telling time except by the sun, moon, or stars. "Stepping about like a rooster," "gaudy as a rooster," "crowing like a rooster," were colorful ways of suggesting pride, arrogance, or flamboyant attire.

Many of the expressions in everyday use in my childhood, however, were rooted deep in the life of the past and made good sense. My parents, in bidding good-bye to departing guests, often said, "Come again. The latchstring is always out." This hospitable remark meant that these friends had a standing invitation to visit at anytime. Knowing the basis for the adage renders it attractive rather than time-worn.

In the 17th and 18th centuries, American colonists were noted for resourcefulness in using available building materials. In the East, we had the log cabin built of trees felled to clear a patch of land for farming. Hardware was not easily obtainable; therefore, the wooden latch was the practical solution for a door fastening. The latch consisted of a stout wooden bar twelve inches in length fastened to the inside of the door. Another bar three or four feet long was constructed to fit into a notch in a similar piece attached to the doorjamb. A cord was secured to the bar and passed through a hole in the door so that the bar could be raised from the outside. This durable cord was usually rawhide, a byproduct of beef slaughtering. It satisfied the frugal instincts of the settlers to let nothing go to waste.

When the cabin door was closed and the latchstring was drawn in, the house was secured against entry. Drawing in the latchstring was the equivalent of locking the door. The opening provided a peephole through which the householder could see the visitor before deciding to open the door. In the days of Indian attacks, the peephole gave the occupants a way of identifying the person outside.

Many fine colonial homes made use of the latchstring as well as the humble cabins of the settlers. "Wakefield," the reconstructed boyhood home of George Washington on the Potomac River, has such a fastening on the front door.

To tell a friend that the latchstring was always out meant that he had free access to the home. In fact, he could lift the latch and walk in without knocking since the string was on the outside.

Today dwellings using the latchstring as a door fastening may be almost non-existent, but the expres-sion lingers. How lovely it is to picture the home owner's door with the latchstring out in welcome to a friend or even a passing traveler! How sad that today we must virtually barricade our homes in an often vain attempt to keep out intruders!

"Don't fly off the handle, Sister" was a caution my mother often uttered to Aunt Gay, who was noted for her quick temper. It is a very strong admonition in view of its literal meaning. The saying also came into our language from the days of the first settlers. Then the axe, hatchet, adz, hoe, and similar tools were a necessity in every household. The blacksmith fashioned the metal head of the tool, and the owner usually made the handle. Hickory was considered the best wood for the purpose, but oak was used also.

The handle was carefully constructed to secure a tight fit. The head was driven onto the handle and a small wooden wedge was often driven in beside it for additional security, because if the head came off the handle, a serious accident might occur. Certainly control of the tool was lost and its usefulness was destroyed, temporarily at least, when this happened.

From time to time, I heard Aunt Gay remark to my father, "The bottom rail is getting on top." I soon realized that this was a rather snobbish comment directed toward someone whose rise to prominence was, she felt, consider-ably above his station in life. The saying was particularly apt in Tidewater, Virginia, where rail fences were common. Farther west where rock fences are found it is not familiar.

The rail fence was used in the eastern United States from colonial days until well into the 20th century. Wood was abundant, labor was cheap, and such fences could be easily constructed, repaired, or moved. These advantages made them especially satisfactory to early settlers. In Virginia, chestnut rails were preferred because they did not rot quickly. A chestnut rail fence would last from twenty to twenty-five years, with only occasional replacement of a deteriorating rail.

Chestnut trees were felled, cut into twelve-foot lengths and split into quarters, eights, or more depending on the size of the tree. A rail should be heavy enough to stay in place but light enough to handle easily. Rails were laid in piles to dry for a year before they were ready for use.

To lay the fence, two sections had to be worked on at the same time; rails were laid in an alternating and zigzag pattern. If they did not fit snugly, a notch could be cut to secure the rails where they crossed. A finished fence was seven rails high. The bottom rail was often chosen for some defect such as a curve or a knot which would not matter as it rested on the earth. Thus the bottom rail had a lowly and unnoticed position.

Often my father would give me a small task to do and if I hesitated, he might reassure me with one of his favorite sayings:

"A short horse is soon curried," an expression straight from the stable.

"Want to feed the corn sheller for me?" He'd ask.

"Oh, Daddy, I haven't time. I haven't finished my homework," I might reply.

"It's a short horse. Come on. You can be back in no time," and, of course, I'd follow him willingly to the barn.

When Marguerite and I squabbled, Mother would reprimand us and conclude her lecture by saying, "Now, bury the hatchet." Apparently this expression goes back

to the Indian practice of burying the tomahawk to denote
the end of hostilities between tribes. To us it was clear
that we must forget our cause of disagreement and
become friends again.

If I accused Marguerite of laziness or jealously, Aunt
Gay would silence me quickly by saying "The pot is
calling the kettle black." The black iron teakettle on the
kitchen range and the black iron pans used for most of
Mother's baking came to mind instantly. They were all
black, and I understood that to Aunt Gay I was as guilty
as Marguerite.

Today the way of life that made these expressions
apt has vanished, and the people who used them and
understood them are a dying breed.

CHAPTER XIV

The Horseless Carriage

I heard it first where I was playing house under the walnut tree. A long continuous rumble, it sounded like far off thunder except that it didn't stop; in fact, it grew louder. What on earth could make a sound like that? I ran to the front gate and climbed the white plank fence to get a view of the road. There was a cloud of dust near the woods and it seemed to be moving toward our house. If it was a buggy, it was making a strange sound, and why couldn't I hear the sound of the horses' hoofbeats? Staring in wonder, I saw a strange vehicle turn from the main road into our lane.

"Mother, Mother," I cried in great excitement, "come quick. There's something coming. Hurry! Hurry!"

At my first cry, my mother ran from the kitchen to join me at the gate.

"It's an automobile. It must be. Runs without horses. Look at it. How fast it's coming!" She was almost as excited as I by the time the queer thing stopped near the gate.

A man wearing a long light coat, which we called a duster, and a flat cap crawled from the machine and came toward us. Mother pulled me to her and waited apprehensively until the man took off his cap and called, "Cousin Kate, are you surprised to see me?"

"Sam Tomlinson, what are you doing driving up in one of those crazy things? Of course, I'm surprised. Come in and tell me what you are doing with an automobile. John will be tickled to see one. He's been reading about them."

She threw her arms around his neck and kissed him, then turned to me. "Louise, this is Cousin Will's brother, Sam, who lives in Baltimore. You've never seen him before. Give him a kiss."

Sam bent down for my kiss and said: "Little Louise, I've heard about you. I've brought you a present." He turned toward the car, and only then did I see the big dog on the back seat. "Come make friends with Prince while I talk to your mother."

I hung back. The dog was different from the hounds and bird dogs that I knew. Cousin Sam untied Prince and he jumped out, a huge terrifying dog, in my eyes, but special. I put out my hand and stroked his fur trying not to look frightened.

"What kind of dog is that, Sam? He's big as a calf." Mother kept her distance; she was not an animal lover like my father and me.

"He's part greyhound and part Belgian shepherd. They are good guard dogs. I thought he would be good to keep thieves away at night." Cousin Sam seemed a trifle uncertain.

Thieves, I thought! What thieves? We never locked a door. We didn't keep the smokehouse locked or the hen houses, and they were the only attraction to the neighborhood poor who might help themselves to a hen or a piece of meat from the smokehouse, but theft was rare. I was puzzled that Cousin Sam would mention such a thing.

"Get your suitcase and come in the house. John will be here for dinner soon. Won't he be surprised to see you and that machine." Mother hurried back to the kitchen with our guest following.

I studied Prince with curiosity and pride. Marguerite would be envious, I thought. He was such a big dog. His head came almost to my shoulder. It was long with a keen muzzle and alert ears that drooped, then pointed forward as if listening to a distant sound. Suddenly Pinky, my cat, came into view and Prince's lips drew back in a snarl to reveal long pointed teeth. I bet people will be afraid of him, I thought. "Nice Prince. Good dog," I said aloud and moved to pat his head. It was then that I noticed his eyes. One was dark but the other was light, a bluish shade with flecks of white. I had never seen such a freak of nature before, and I was startled but instantly sympathetic. Poor thing, I thought, one blue eye is bad but I have two. (Remember, blue eyes, in my mother's judgment did not rate as high as brown.)

"I think you're beautiful anyway," I told him and conquering my fears, I threw my arms around his neck and hugged him. He pressed against me and wagged his tail. Our friendship was sealed. From then on Prince was my shadow and I was his champion. We seemed to develop an empathy that had not existed between Snowball and me, much as I had loved the little mongrel.

"Are you hungry, Prince? Come on, I'll find you something to eat," I promised.

He waited for me at the kitchen door until I returned with a big piece of bread. He smelled it and finally accepted it. He did not gulp it down as Marguerite's brother's hounds would have done but lay down with it between his paws and ate daintily.

"Is that your new dog, Baby?" said Auntie coming to the door to look at him. "He's too big for a little girl like you, isn't he?"

"No, he's not. I think he's beautiful. He really looks like a prince. See; he's already my friend," I answered as she watched the dog lift his head to nuzzle against my arm.

"Well, he is majestic, I guess," she replied as Prince got to his feet and rose to his full height. "I hope he fits in here on the farm."

"He will." I responded blithely with no premonition of his troubled days or tragic death in a few months.

When my father came to dinner, he was astounded to see an automobile in the front yard. He and the two hired men, Connie and Charles, walked around it, studying it from every angle.

"Where de hitch de horses, Mis' Shubank, I don't see no single-tree or buggy pole?" asked Connie deeply puzzled.

"It runs on gasoline not horse power. I've read about them." My father turned to greet Cousin Sam who had come from the house to speak to him. After shaking hands, the men looked at the car again and my father said, "I want to see it run. Maybe Mr. Sam will give you a ride later," but Charles and Connie looked dubious and shook their heads.

After dinner was over, Cousin Sam was eager to show off his new vehicle. Even Mother approved of the running board upon which one stepped to enter the car and the doors which closed to give a protected feeling to the occupants. Cousin Sam lifted the hood which covered the motor and pointed out parts of the engine to the admiring gaze of my father and the two hired men. Then he adjusted the gauges, took up a strange-looking bent handle, came to the front of the machine, inserted it in a hole under the front grill, and spun the crank vigorously. With a loud splutter the engine caught and roared into life. Charles and Connie, who had inched closer and closer, turned and raced for the barn. My mother and I stood behind a tree, but my father watched fascinated as Cousin Sam climbed behind the steering wheel.

"Come on, John, you and Cousin Kate can go for a ride," he yelled over the rumble of the motor.

"No. No," my mother was pale with fright. "I'm scared to death of the thing. John, come away from it before you get hurt."

"Pshaw, Kate, if it doesn't hurt Sam, it won't hurt me," replied my father laughing as he gave her a reassuring hug. "Of course, I want to ride. Baby, if your mother won't go, how about you?" My father stepped forward and so did I.

"Louise, you haven't a grain of sense," Mother said. "Come back here this minute. If your father hasn't any better sense than to get into that thing I can't stop him, but you better mind me." Her tone and manner convinced me that argument was useless.

Charles and Connie crept from the barn to watch my father ride off.

"Ain't dat somepun! Mis' Shubank ain't scared of nothing," said Connie admiringly. Charles looked as if he agreed with my mother's assessment of my father, but he said nothing. The automobile chugged away with its occupants and passed out of sight while we waited in anxiety until it returned.

Cousin Sam left the next morning to return to his home. His visit had brought excitement to our lives which lasted for days.

After he had gone, my mother told me why he had come. His only son, Bruce, had died a few weeks before with a ruptured appendix. Prince had been Bruce's dog and he and his wife, in their distress, felt that they must find a home for him. Cousin Sam had thought of our big old farm with its menagerie of animals and had brought the dog to us hoping we would keep him.

"He's a city dog, John. Never been in the country before. He's not used to pigs and chickens, horses and cows," he'd told my father. "You'll have to train him, but he's smart; he'll learn quick. I hope he won't be any trouble."

"Don't worry, Sam. We'll look after him, and Louise needs a dog." My little pet, Snowball, which Mother said was so ugly that he was cute, had died of distemper two months before and I had missed him sorely. My father thought that it was time I had another dog. Of course, he had no idea of the difficulties ahead.

Cousin Sam's visit left a deep desire in my father to own an automobile. He was sure the horseless carriage was the future form of transportation, and he wanted one.

"Give me the old horse and buggy every time," my mother announced as we drove to church next Sunday. "These automobiles will never do away with the horse. I'm surprised that Sam would waste his money buying one."

"You may be wrong, Kate," said Auntie. "Those things will be improved and developed until they are comfortable and safe, I think. I can see it coming."

"Safe! Nonsense. It'll never be safe," replied Mother. "What could it do on roads like these? It may run all right now in dry weather, but it would be mired in a minute in bad weather."

"Roads will have to be improved, of course, but think what it would mean in time saved," answered Auntie. "John, would you be willing to give up your surrey for a car?" Aunt Gay turned to my father who had listened to the discussion without comment so far.

"Well, I'll tell you one thing," he replied with such emphasis that my mother kept quiet, "I expect to own one by the time Louise is ready for college."

I snuggled closer to him. We will own a car, and I will ride in it, I thought, still disappointed in not having ridden with Cousin Sam when I had the chance. My father and I understood each other; we were both dreamers.

His words were prophetic for we did indeed buy a car, a Model T Ford, the spring that I finished high school. By that time I had become quite accustomed to them, but my mother was still apprehensive. She rode for sometime with the door unfastened, holding it together with her hand, in case she should want to get out. Aunt Gay, however, sat solidly in the back seat and enjoyed the 35 mile-an-hour speed as we rolled along.

CHAPTER XV

The Death of Prince

For the first few days after Prince came to live with us, he kept to himself except when I was outside; then he followed me everywhere. He seemed to have transferred his affection from his dead master to me and was now definitely my dog. He found a place to sleep under the front porch where he was out of the way of the farm animals; I put an old rug there for a bed, and he appeared satisfied.

As soon as he felt at home things changed. First, he began to chase the hens in what appeared to be a spirit of playfulness. When he caught one, he would hold the poor frightened thing down with his paw and lick it.

"Prince, let that hen alone," my father would shout and the dog would slink away, cowed and ashamed, but the temptation was too great and soon he would be at it again. When chasing hens became tame, he tried to chase Pinky, my cat, who promptly climbed a tree. The dog sat below the tree patiently waiting for her to come down until I called him to follow me; but next time Pinky stood her ground and gave him a sharp-clawed slap which surprised him and taught him a lesson. He never bothered her again.

His next misdemeanor was making a bed in Mother's dahlia border. He knocked over and broke off three of her named varieties of dahlias and incurred her wrath. She had hit him sharply with a switch, and he had run off in disgrace.

"You'll just have to give him a good whipping, John," said Aunt Gay when this escapade was told at the supper table.

My family believed in the Biblical proverb: Spare the rod and spoil the child, as I well knew. Chastisement was the usual method of training animals as well as children, and I was sure that Prince would get it sooner or later.

Not long after this, Uncle Richie came by one morning to tell us that Prince had chased a young calf in his barn lot.

"That city dog of yours doesn't belong in the country, Louise," he said jokingly, but I knew he meant it. This was serious; we could not allow our animals to bother other people. It would lead to hard feelings between our families.

"I guess I'll have to tie him up or get rid of him," my father said after Uncle had gone.

"He's a city dog, Daddy. He didn't know he shouldn't play with the calf, and he'd hate being tied. Please don't do it yet," I pled.

Unfortunately, Prince was popular with no one but me. Marguerite made fun of him, but I understood that. She usually undervalued anything that belonged to me. He was too big, she didn't like his blue eye, his bark sounded like a bullfrog, and he scared her kittens, she said. Anyway, what would anybody want with a city dog? She had nothing to say in his favor.

In addition, the hired helpers on the place were suspicious of him.

"Dat dog no good, Mister John," said Connie. "Look at dat ebil eye. He hooked up wid de debbil, for sho."

"Don't let dat dog come 'round me. I'se scared to deaf of him," exclaimed Mary, Mother's kitchen helper. "I don't want him looking at me wid dat eye. He put a spell on you. You better leave him be, Louise."

"Oh, Mary, he can't help his blue eye. He's gentle and wouldn't hurt anybody," I cried, but they all said, "git him away from me," so I kept him with me as much as possible.

When school opened and I was away all day, I couldn't look after Prince, so I was not surprised to find him tied and straining at the rope when I came home one afternoon.

I hurried to find my father to ask if I could untie him. Daddy was shucking corn in a field near the house.

"Come here, Louise. I want to talk to you," he said as I approached. "I have some bad news for you. Prince has been sucking eggs."

Prince a suck-egg dog! How could my beautiful Prince be a suck-egg dog!

This was a serious crime, next to killing sheep. Eggs were important in a farm household not only for food, but also for barter. When Mother sent to the store for grocery items, she always sent a basket of eggs to pay for them. We seldom spent hard cash for the sugar, coffee, tea, soda, or baking powder that we needed. If eggs were plentiful, we lived a little better than when they were scarce. I was familiar with this system and was given an egg to spend for candy when the supply was abundant. Candy from the store was a real treat and I hoarded the two or three lemon drops an egg bought. Loss of eggs meant more than fewer for breakfast.

"Are you sure he's sucking eggs? How do you know?" I asked in real dismay.

"I found him in the nest in the hay barn. He had egg yolk on his mouth and bits of shell in his teeth. He's been doing this a good while, I'm sure, because we haven't been getting as many eggs as we ought. No, honey, it's no mistake." Daddy's voice was serious, and I knew Prince was in grave danger.

"If I keep him with me, can I untie him for a little while now, please?"

"Yes, but tie him again when you go into the house," he replied.

As we played I worried. What was to become of my dog? To keep him tied was a poor life for an animal, and everyone said it was impossible to break a dog from sucking eggs, once he started. Could I find a home for him with someone who didn't live on a farm? I thought of Cousin Pearl, who lived in Urbanna and of Dick Brooks whose Dad kept store at Centerville, but I said nothing.

Everyday, when I came from school, Prince would be lying, woebegone and listless, where he was tied and I would loose him for a romp. One afternoon I found only the rope and empty collar. The dog was gone. I called and he came promptly running out from under the front porch where he liked to sleep.

"Have you been a bad dog, Princie? You haven't eaten eggs, have you?" I questioned and hugged him as he gave me a straight-forward look. His majestic stance and loving attitude convinced me that he could do no wrong. He followed me as I brought in wood for the cookstove and pumped three buckets of water, but I tied him when I went to gather eggs.

"Sorry, Princie. Sorry, but I have to," I apologized as I tightened the collar and wondered why he had been loose. Next day it was the same. I sought my mother.

"Somebody is untying Prince everyday. Why is that?" I asked, but she knew nothing and neither did my father when I inquired of him.

A few days later the puzzle was solved. I saw Prince pull his head through the collar, and I realized that a collar which was not too tight to choke him could slip over his long, narrow head.

"Guess I'll have to build him a dog house then," said my father when I told him, but before he could get around to it, Prince disappeared.

Seeing the empty collar Tuesday afternoon when I returned from school, I knew what had happened. He's done it again, I thought.

"Here, Prince. Here, Prince," I called but he did not come. I set about my chores, calling and looking for him everywhere I went. Dark came but he did not appear.

"Daddy, what do you think has happened to him?" I asked when I found him milking Princess at the barn.

"I have no idea. He generally stays around the house, doesn't he?" my father seemed perplexed but he reassured me. "He'll show up soon, I guess."

But the next morning when I left for school at 7:00 a.m., Prince had not come home and was not there when I returned. I began to cry when I couldn't find him. Mother and Auntie were sympathetic and suggested that I go to play with Marguerite in an attempt to get my mind off the dog's disappearance.

"She won't care where he is. She doesn't like him. None of you liked him. Your're glad he's gone," I sobbed. "Why doesn't somebody go to look for him? He may be caught in a trap and can't get out." I knew that my cousin Dick had traps set for muskrats in the marsh, and it was entirely possible that Prince had wandered into one. The thought of Prince suffering brought more tears.

"As soon as Daddy gets back from the store, he'll go to look for him," promised Mother. "Don't cry so, Baby, we'll find him. Just wait."

By the time my father rode in, I was almost in hysterics. He tried to comfort me, but he seemed uncomfortable.

"I'll ride up to Connie's house and see if he knows anything," he said.

"Let me go with you, please," I begged but Daddy said no, he was on horseback and I couldn't go.

He was gone sometime and, when he returned, I knew as soon as I saw his face that he had bad news.

"Prince is dead," he told me as Mother and Aunt Gay listened. "Come here, Baby, and I'll tell you what happened." I crawled into his lap, buried my face in his shoulder, and cried piteously as he tried to explain.

"You know, Louise, that we couldn't keep him tied. He kept getting loose and he'd eat every egg he could find. I didn't want to get rid of him because he was your dog and you loved him. I was trying to decide what to do. Last week when Charles was here cutting wood, I said to him when we walked by Prince 'I'll give you 25 cents to kill that dog.' I really didn't expect him to do it with no more instructions than that, and I didn't think anymore about it until the dog couldn't be found. I've just been to Charles' house, and he says he killed him two days ago. It is my fault, and I'm sorry, Baby."

As I heard these words I drew back, struggled from his arms, though he tried to hold me, and looked him full in the face.

"YOU killed my dog! Daddy, how could you! I'll never forgive you." With these harsh words I rushed from the room and ran upstairs to my bed, where I cried in great hiccoughing sobs. I finally became quiet as it grew dark. At last Auntie came in with a lighted lamp in her hand. She set it carefully on the bureau and came to the bed.

"We are all so sorry about Prince, darling. Your father feels worst of all. He didn't mean what he said to Charles. He wants you to come down to supper now and try to think about something else. Tomorrow he'll find his body and bury it. Come on now; I know you're hungry." Aunt Gay had been stroking my hair in her gentlest way and her voice was trembling.

I wiped my eyes and went with her, but I had nothing to say to anyone. I didn't even thank Daddy for doing my chores for me. As he rose from the table, Daddy came over to me and put his hand on my shoulder.

"Louise, I never intended this to happen. Please forgive me. I'll get you another dog."

"No," I answered stonily, shrugging away his hand. "I'll never have another dog. Never."

The next day Daddy sent Charles to bury Prince's body. When he returned, he brought the collar, and Daddy gave it to me. I took it, carried it to my room, wrapped it carefully in tissue paper, and put it in the bottom bureau drawer where it stayed for years. I did not ask where the grave was nor did I go to see it.

It was a week before anyone told me the full story of Prince's death. Then Aunt Gay gave me the details. Charles had taken my father at his word, had untied Prince, and had coaxed him to follow him into the woods. He had cut a sapling some ten feet in length, and when they came to a deep place in the Exol stream, he had tied the dog to it and thrown him into the water, not even staying to see what happened. "A powerful dog like Prince must have struggled there for hours unable to get out with the long pole tied to him. Your father was so angry when he heard what Charles had done, that he went to the stream to look for the dog, thinking he might have gotten out and be still living, but he drowned. That's why he was so long in getting back home that afternoon," explained Aunt Gay.

It was an agonizing picture that formed in my mind. I hated Charles for his act, and I had not forgiven my father for his part in the sad story. Now the details made it worse. I had accepted the fact of Prince's death—I had lost pets before—but to me this death was totally unnecessary. Farm children are not insulated from death as many modern children are. It was routine to kill chickens and pigs for food, cows were sent to market, pets died, and relatives and people in the community passed away. Children saw the dead, attended funerals, and knew that death was an inevitable part of life. The death of Prince caused the first rift between my father and me, and it became both wide and deep.

I resisted every effort he made to make up. I brought in wood, pumped water, gathered eggs, performed my assigned tasks, but I did not hang about the barn as before just to be with him. When we drove to church in the surrey, I asked Aunt Gay if I could sit in back with her, and my mother rode in the front seat. My coolness relaxed a little as the months passed, but my hurt did not go away. As far as Charles was concerned, I refused to notice him. When he was working about the place, it was as though he were invisible. Mother and Aunt Gay talked to me. Holding a grudge was bad. "Forgive and forget," they said.

I replied, "yes m'am," politely, but I did not relent.

Finally in late spring I came home from school one day to find my father waiting for me. This was unusual. He was generally busy somewhere about the place, but he was standing at the well and apparently watching for me. We entered the kitchen together, and I stopped at the pie safe for something to eat, a long established habit. He went into the dining room where Mother and Aunt Gay were and called, "Come here, Louise, I've something to show you."

Pushing open the swinging door between the rooms, I started in. There in the middle of the room was the most adorable collie puppy I had ever seen. His black eyes were bright in his pointed face framed by delicate white ruff; his ears were raised, alert to the new sounds, and his tail wagged madly. He was utterly irresistible. Gone were my memories of Prince. I uttered a cry of joy and swept the puppy up into my arms, burying my face in his fluffy coat.

"He's for you, Louise. Do you like him?"

"Oh, Daddy, I love him. Is he really mine?"

"Yes, of course. Can you think of a good name for him?"

"Laddie, he's going to be Laddie. Isn't that a good name?" I turned to Mother for her reaction. Her eyes were shining as she nodded, and Aunt Gay was smiling.

"It's just right," said my father.

Then I lifted my face for Daddy's kiss and threw my arm around his neck, the puppy a wriggling ball between us. The rift was healed at last.

Laddie soon filled the spot in my heart left vacant by Prince's death. He grew to be a handsome, useful dog on the farm and remained a part of our family, living out a pampered old age, until long after I was grown.

Louise and Laddie

CHAPTER XVI

Dining Days

Christmas week was the period between Christmas Day and New Year's Day. It was a time of relaxation from farm work, except for the necessary care of the stock for the men, and it was marked by a succession of dining days. At Christmas time the emphasis was on food, food, and more food. Families entertained each other, vying for a day "when you can come to our house." On these occasions we gorged ourselves on every delicacy available, although there was great sameness in the menus from house to house.

The planning began days ahead at our home. The big turkey strutting about the barnyard was earmarked as the Christmas turkey; the two-year old ham hanging in the smokehouse had already been designated as the Christmas ham. These were standard items on the menu. The ham was my father's specialty. He did not smoke it, as many did, but cured it with saltpeter, black pepper, and salt.

"How do you cure your hams, John?" someone at the table would be sure to ask, and he would launch into a detailed account of the process.

"Not too much salt," he would say. "Salt makes the meat hard. The black pepper keeps out flies, and the saltpeter gives the meat its red color. I trim off most of the fat to give the ham a good shape."

"I smoke mine with hickory wood," Cousin Robbie would say, and the discussion of methods of curing meat would have the full attention of the men at the table. The women might be sharing recipes for pound cake.

Some items could be made far in advance. The Christmas fruit cake was made before Thanksgiving in many households. A pound cake, made two week before the date, kept very well in a lard tin on the back porch. Molasses and sugar candy could be made early, and, of course, pickles and preserves had been sitting on the pantry shelf since summer. As the date approached, Mother began the final preparations.

"John, bring me the ham from the smokehouse this morning, please. You know the one, the biggest. We will have two dinings next week. It won't be too much," my mother announced.

"All right. I'll put it in soak for you so you can cook it tomorrow. Did I tell you that John Temple won't be peddling oysters this year? He's been sick and can't get to the river to tong them. I'll have to go to Bowlers to get some myself," replied my father.

"Better go Thursday then, I guess. I have my list of groceries for you to get at Center Cross and I can't make my coconut cake until you buy the coconuts," answered Mother.

"Please let me go with you when you go to the store, Daddy. I want to see what Mr. Newbill has for Christmas this year." I saw a chance for an exciting trip.

"No, Louise. I'll have to drive the wagon to Bowlers. I can't bring back two bushels of oysters and all the other things in the buggy. It will be too long a trip for you anyway. I wish I could take you though." Daddy never refused me if he could help it, because he knew opportunities for outings were few.

My father would return from his trip to the river with the oysters and laden with fresh coconuts, lemons, oranges, raisins, a bag of mixed nuts, and pounds of sugar from the store.

I loved to sort through the nuts identifying the different kinds: pale, straw-colored almonds with a slightly bitter flavor; shiny, round hazelnuts with a brown spot at one end and a neat little point at the other; long, pointed, light-brown pecans; and, best of all, the fat gray Brazil nuts, "nigger-toes," we called them. Largest of the nuts, oily and rich, they were an unusual treat to me. These nuts were for eating, and some would go into the stocking I hung on the mantel on Christmas Eve. We had an abundance of black walnuts for general use. They were wonderful for candy and cake frostings, but they offered special problems of their own.

The black walnut is encased in a green hull that turns brown as it ripens. This has to be removed before the hard, rough shell that encloses the meat can be cracked. "Hulling walnuts" by hand left the hands stained brown for weeks. Many children came to school with brown hands from Thanksgiving until Christmas. The walnut hull was the source of the brown dye used by the colonists, and a good source it was, because it was impossible to wash out; it had to wear away. The hard shell defied a nut cracker; it had to be cracked with a hammer against a very hard substance, an up-ended oak block, a rock, or any old piece of iron. Picking out the meat was slow too, but Aunt Gay loved this job. She would sit for an hour with a big pan of cracked shells, munching on choice tidbits as she worked, and being accused jokingly of eating more than she saved.

The coconuts, gathered from some far off tropical shore, were a special part of Christmas to me. I pictured the palm trees bending under the huge fruit and wondered what it would be like actually to pick some myself. I had never seen the coconut before its outer covering was removed, and my mental picture was all wrong because I saw them growing like apples amid the palm fronds. The coarse brown shells with the three "eyes" or soft spots were so different, both in appearance and flavor, from other fruits, that they were in a class by themselves.

Preparing coconut for use was tedious. First, two soft spots had to be punctured and the nut balanced over a small bowl or glass to drain off the milk inside. The slow drip of the milk ended, the hard outer shell had to be cracked, and oily, white meat pried from the shell. Next the brown covering on the meat had to be peeled away with a sharp knife leaving a number of irregular sized pieces to be grated. My father usually took over the latter job because it took strong fingers to hold the pieces and rub them against the jagged grater. Often a piece would slip and leave a grated knuckle as a result. At long last a bowl of grated coconut would be ready for use, and I would be allowed to eat the pieces too small to grate.

Mother's coconut cake was a Christmas favorite. She baked 1-2-3-4 cake batter (one cup butter, two cups sugar, three cups flour, four eggs) in layers and frosted them with seven-minute icing to which generous amounts of grated coconut had been added. Gold and white, moist and delicate, this cake was fit for the gods. Another coconut delight was a rich, custard pie. And then there were the "shapes." These were really little individual pies; the pie crust was rolled, cut into circles, and fitted into muffin tins. The filling was a mixture of eggs, butter, sugar, and coconut baked in the crust. She made lemon ones, too, in a similar fashion. There were dozens of shapes for between meal snacks. When they visited, my cousins, Dick, William, and George, would each take three or four to tide them over until meal time. Sometimes a plate piled high with the dainty pies would be offered to company who dropped in.

Ambrosia made with fresh oranges and coconut was tangy and luscious. This dessert, the ultimate in extravagance, was served only at Christmas because this was the only time we were apt to have either fruit. Fresh coconut desserts are not unknown today, but few housewives will spend the time to prepare the coconut. The packaged or frozen kind will make a good dessert, but nothing compares with the freshly grated coconut.

Mince pie was another dessert for the season. Mincemeat was made in the fall when someone in the neighborhood killed a beef. A piece of lean beef and suet was boiled until it fell apart. The beef was chopped into tiny pieces (minced) and added to fresh chopped apples, raisins, and spices, and the mixture cooked to a thick consistency, sending out tantalizing odors as it boiled that made me drool. The mince meat was then canned to be ready for some important occasion. (I often asked for it on my birthday, December 30; to me it was better than cake.) Mince pie, warm from the oven, with a splash of whiskey on it, was always received with delight, but my father, who was a faithful "teetotaler," made us leave off the whiskey when someone told him he was breaking the prohibition law.

When Mother served mince pie, some guest was sure to inquire. "Kate, why didn't you set the broom in the corner so we'd know something this good was coming?" referring to a custom of alerting the family with the broom when there was dessert to follow. No one ever refused dessert, however. Hearty appetites were expected. I never heard of anyone who watched calories or dieted unless the doctor ordered it for a serious ailment.

The prohibition law apparently did not include wine jelly; we served it with no protests. It was a colorful, light dessert to serve after a heavy meal. Brought to the table in sherbet glasses, its ruby-red planes reflecting the lamplight, and topped with snowy cap of whipped cream, it was the perfect accompaniment for cake.

Boiled custard was also part of Christmas. Fresh milk was scalded and poured over beaten eggs and sugar. The mixture was returned to the stove to cook until thickened; then it was seasoned with vanilla and chilled before serving. Thick, smooth, creamy, and sprinkled with nutmeg, it came to the table in punch cups with a pitcher to provide seconds. Some people served it over wine jelly, but not so in our household. The combination seemed to lessen the appeal of each and to produce second-rate dessert.

Most of the delicacies I have described were made ahead of the actual dining day and stored in a safe cold place. As Christmas week approached, the activity in the kitchen increased. It was time to cook the ham. It had to be scraped, washed, and soaked over night. On the day it was cooked, the heavy iron ham boiler took up most of the cooking surface on the range. The ham was covered with water and cooked just below boiling point for hours, until the end bone was loose, and it "stuck tender." To keep a slow fire required careful attention to the amount of wood put into the stove; a few pieces at a time to keep the fire burning without going out did the trick. The monster of a ham was cooled in the cooking water, possibly over night. Next day it was skinned, trimmed, garnished with cloves and molasses, and browned in the oven.

A more elegant dish than the ham ready for the table is hard to imagine. Then, with all possible preparations made, we awaited the beginning of dining days. Ours would come two days after Christmas Day which we usually spent with my father's sister, my Aunt Byrd. This had been her regular time for years, and no one attempted to change it.

A day or so before Christmas, my father and I would search out a thick bushy cedar along the fence rows, cut it, and bring it home to decorate. Our ornaments were carefully saved from year to year; we used tinsel too, but of course, no lights. The tree was taken down before New Year's; it was bad luck to have it up after the New Year began.

I always hung up my stocking (really one of Daddy's socks which would hold more) on Christmas Eve and would find it filled to overflowing next morning, and there were other gifts beneath the Christmas tree as well. My presents were usually practical; I loved clothes, so a coat or a new dress delighted me. However, I had plenty of dolls, books, and games, and I still treasure a Noritake (Nippon) tea set that I received when I was ten. We exchanged gifts with relatives, but they were never wrapped in gorgeous paper tied with enormous bows as they are today, when the wrappings may outdo the contents of the package. Gifts were often handmade. I remember giving my mother a purple velvet pin cushion (probably made by Aunt Gay) on which I had outlined her initial, a capital K, in straight pins. I thought the effect of the shining pins against the rich purple was handsome, and so did she.

Our customary breakfast on Christmas morning was crackling bread and stewed oysters. After the excitement of opening packages, my father would go to the smoke-house where the oysters were stored, with a big bowl and his oyster knife. Each shell had to be pried open with the blade of the knife, and the oyster cut loose from its attachment to the shell. Daddy would flip each one into the bowl with a quick snap of his wrist. When the quantity was sufficient, he would come back into the kitchen, stamping his cold feet and blowing on his cold fingers. There might even be ice in the bowl of oysters. The crackling bread which Mother had prepared while the oysters were being opened was baking in the oven. It was a rich mixture of corn meal, salt, and cracklings, the crisp bits of fat left after lard had been rendered. Mixed with water and formed into oval cakes about an inch thick, it came from the oven brown, crisp, and delectable. The stew, a combination of oyster broth, fresh milk and butter with plump oysters floating in it, would be brought to the table in a large tureen to be ladled into soup bowls. As the cover was lifted, the steam curled upward from the hot liquid, and the tantalizing smell of crackling bread mingled with the delicate aroma of oysters. I could hardly wait for the blessing which was lengthened in recognition of the day. My father thanked God for the gift of His Son, for the bounty of the food before us, and for the joy of a united, happy family. How blessed we were indeed!

As soon as we could, we would be on our way, with hot bricks at our feet and wrapped in blankets against the cold, for Aunt Byrd's, the first of the succession of dining days. There would be a large crowd at "Pleasant Grove," a mingling of four families, at least. The custom there was for the men and older boys to go hunting after the crowd had assembled. They straggled off to the woods with two or three dogs in search of any game they might find. The women gathered in the kitchen and dining room offering to help with the preparations, but some, finding themselves in the way, would congregate in the parlor. The girls and younger children would find an empty bedroom and begin a fascinating conversation about what we had received for Christmas. The time passed quickly, and soon we would hear a yelping of dogs and see the men returning, guns on their arms, and maybe a squirrel or a rabbit to show for their trouble. The hunt had not been a serious search for game, but a way of passing the time and working up an appetite to do justice to the over-abundance of food prepared for them.

There would be three tables at least. Priority was determined by age. The older generation went to the table to sample the delectable array of food first. The second table would be made up of the next generation, the young married couples, who were more relaxed with their dignified elders out of the way. There would be joking, teasing, and great fellowship among this group. A dish washing operation would start as soon as they left the table to have plates and cutlery for the crowd of hungry children still waiting. When all had been fed, the food removed, the dishes washed and put away, it would be time for the sweet course. The sumptuous pies, cakes, jelly, and custard would be brought out, and the three groups served in rotation as before. The process took up the whole day. The hostess would have had no time to mingle with her guests except those who came to her aid. Even with a colored maid in the kitchen, it was a mammoth undertaking to host a dining day, but the housewives looked forward with eagerness to this opportunity to entertain, to show off their cooking, and to reciprocate for similar days which they had enjoyed elsewhere.

As the winter day waned, horses would be hitched to the various vehicles for the return drive home. We often arrived after dark because we lived the farthest away. Uncomplaining, my father would change his clothes, light the lantern, get his milk buckets, and go to the barn to do chores. There was no leaving things off to be done the next day. A farmer had to practice discipline on many occasions.

The next morning would see us off in another direction, to my mother's brother's this time. Here the routine was much the same except that the group was smaller, and no one went hunting. The men congregated in the parlor, the children in a bedroom, and the women in the dining room and kitchen. It was at one of these gatherings that an episode took place that made a lasting impression on both Marguerite and me.

The children gathered that day were all old enough to require no adult supervision. George, William, Virginia, Marguerite, Temple Lee, and I were busily telling about our gifts and examining each other's presents. We were all wearing or carrying something just received for Christmas.

"Look't this knife. It has three blades and, boy, is it ever sharp. Feel that blade." George was passing his favorite gift from one to the other for their admiration. "Mind, don't cut yourself. It's so sharp you could cut your finger off," he warned.

"Is that your new dress, Virginia? I love the color. Santa Claus bring you that?" asked Marguerite of our cousin Virginia, who tossed her head and laughed.

"You think Santa Claus brought this down the chimney? Don't be silly. My mother and father gave me this. I have new shoes too," and she pointed at some black pumps.

"What did you get, William?" asked Temple Lee.

"A shot gun. It's upstairs in my room. I don't want you all putting your hands on it. It's too dangerous." William was the oldest of the crowd and thought himself too big for this childishness, and yet he did not want to be left out.

"What did you get, Louise?" asked Virginia, but before I could answer Marguerite cut me off.

"Oh, now she's going to show off her new dress and her RING. Haven't you seen it yet? The way she's been waving her hand around."

"Louise, you got a ring! Show it to us," cried Temple Lee and Virginia while George came closer to look.

"Here it is. It's a chip diamond." I held my hand out and pointed to a modest little ring on my left hand with a tiny set in it. It was my prized possession that day, and I was glowing with pride.

"Diamond! Nothing but a piece of glass," Marguerite declared laughing gleefully.

Stung, I turned on her. "It is so a diamond. It came from Richmond. My Uncle Archie sent it to me, and he said it was a diamond," I answered hotly.

Marguerite came over to me, pointed to my ring, and repeated her insulting statement.

"A piece of window pane!" and she laughed.

There was a sharp, clear sound—a bit like a window pane breaking. Marguerite gasped, Virginia and Temple Lee stared incredulously. It was the sound of a slap. I stood transfixed. My hand had acted on its own volition. There was the print of my hand on her cheek. The stillness lasted only a split second; then Marguerite's wail of surprise and pain brought our mothers on the run. What had happened? Louise had slapped Marguerite! Unthinkable!

My mother led me away in shame and humiliation. To think that her daughter would forget her training, would stoop to such an unladylike act, would do a thing so crude and unmannerly as to SLAP her own dear little cousin. She would never get over it! What on earth made me do such a thing?

"She said my diamond was a piece of window pane. It's not so. She told a lie," I answered unrepentant and still angry.

"Louise, a lady does not use the word LIE. That is a vulgar way to speak. Never let me hear you say such a thing again." Mother was finding the situation growing worse by the minute. "Come and apologize to Marguerite this instant," she ordered.

"No. She did tell a story. I won't apologize."

"Louise, you will sit here by yourself unless you are ready to say you're sorry and can behave like a lady. Come." Mother rose to leave, but I stood still. She left the room and closed the door.

In the distance I could hear the sounds of dishes rattling, people talking, and happy laughter, but I sat alone. The afternoon waned, and at last my father came for me.

"It's time to go home, Baby. Come and get your coat and tell Marguerite you are sorry."

"But I would be telling a story, Daddy. I can't do that. You said never, never tell something that's not true, and I'm not sorry I slapped her. She made fun of me, and my ring is not a piece of window pane. I know it isn't."

Faced with such a dilemma, my father repeated that we must go home. I told everyone goodbye and climbed into the surrey. I hid my hand with the ring on it in my muff and tried to look unconcerned. Aunt Gay, my faithful champion, invited me to ride in back with her, and I accepted. When we were out of sight of the house, she opened her handbag and pulled out two ham biscuits and a large piece of cake and slipped them into my lap. Starved, I gobbled them gratefully. I'm sure Mother and Daddy knew what was going on, but they took no notice.

The next day was our big dining and the morning was taken up with cooking the turkey, padding oysters to be fried, arranging the table, keeping up fires, drawing water, and a multitude of errands. No one referred to my terrible lapse of the previous day. When Marguerite arrived, she was all smiles and admired my Parchesi game and offered to play when I could get a chance.

The incident was never referred to again, but Marguerite, from that day on, treated me with a measure of respect.

Dining days were held on a less elaborate scale at other times during the year. A favorite time for a gathering of relatives would be after church on a pretty Sunday in the spring or fall, or to celebrate a birthday. My father's Aunt Ella loved to invite her children (we were included in this group) to "go home to dinner" with her after church. On a typical fall Sunday a procession of buggies and surreys would leave for the two mile drive to the home of Uncle Bob and Aunt Ella. Under the blazing gum and poplar trees, across a little stream with fallen leaves floating in the water, where the horses stopped to drink, we would make our slow way. The day provided an opportunity for the men to talk farming, for the women to discuss housekeeping problems, and for the young cousins to get acquainted. Dining days strengthened the family bond.

CHAPTER XVII

Jack and Jill

"Here you are, Louise," Aunt Het opened her apron and handed me two just-hatched greenish yellow balls of fluff. "Maude McGinnis' goslings. If they take after her, they'll make good pets." Her gnarled hands cradled the little birds gently.

"O-ooh, thank you." I reached to take them trembling with excitement.

My delight must have been written on my homely little face because Aunt Het was smiling too. Then she admonished somewhat sternly.

"Now treat'em right, or I'll take'em back." Perhaps she had become suddenly afraid that she had entrusted something precious to one too young and irresponsible for the task.

"I will. Oh, I will," I promised and ran home in ecstasy to show my mother the beautiful present I had received.

By the time I had climbed the stile, jumped to the other side of the fence, sprinted across the field to arrive breathless at the kitchen door, I had named the goslings Jack and Jill. Alike as two peas, they were indistinguishable so I did not know for months which was Jack and which was Jill.

Mother greeted me with resignation. She was used to my succession of pets. I always had a few kittens and Laddie, the family collie, was a fast friend. Spring usually brought a bird fallen from a nest, a baby rabbit, or a chicken. I even rescued baby mice when Daddy found a nest cleaning out the grain barn, though the cat usually got them, but I had never had a pet gosling, and oh, how I had wanted one!

Of all young fowls goslings are the easiest to tame. They are instant charmers. Just out of the nest, they are covered with thick, downy fluff of a deep golden sheen if the feathers are to be white, or of a rich greenish-gold cast if they are to be gray. Their eyes are shiny black beads, their bills bright yellow, carrying the hint of a smile, and their big flat feet are orange. Their most appealing characteristic, however, is the voice. Goslings talk in the gentlest and sweetest of tones, melodious, expressive, and loving.

Mother and I found a suitable box for Jack and Jill and placed it on the porch in the sunshine where they nestled close together. I hung over them most of the day and talked to them constantly. In a few hours they were ready to leave the box and follow at my heels like a dog.

Next day, my father located a coop that would do, and we set up their domicile under the big walnut tree where I could keep watch over them. Laddie accepted them easily too as a part of the household that he was supposed to guard. Every night after they had gone to bed, I closed the door to the coop with bricks so that weasels could not get in and destroy them. We also had to be on guard against rats that would burrow under the floor of the coop.

All summer Jack and Jill wandered about the yard talking to me in dulcet tones, whenever I came near, and nipping the tender green grass. Geese graze almost like cattle or sheep. A flock of ten or fifteen geese can keep a grass lot short almost as well as sheep. They are selective

eaters and will eat weeds without harming certain cultivated plants. For this reason, they can be used as
weeders. Aunt Het depended on her geese to keep weeds
out of her strawberries, but I kept mine strictly as pets.
They were big eaters and loved the biscuits I brought
them frequently, and they would eat out of my hands as I
sat on the kitchen steps. They would cock their heads, fix
their bright eyes on me, and chatter in their soft voices as
I talked to them. We were great companions.

They grew to full size, gave up their baby ways, and
paced sedately about the yard or sat under the shade of
the lilac bush in aloof silence on hot days. Jack and Jill
were a pair. As Jack grew more authoritative and Jill more
submissive, their sex was revealed. Because I spent so
much time with them, they did not mingle much with the
other fowls. They ate with the poultry night and morning, but they were content to share their coop at night
and enjoy their own society.

Geese mate for life. Oscar, the gander, and Maude
McGinnis, parents of my pets, had shared life together in
Aunt Hettie's barnyard menagerie for several years. In
nesting season Oscar kept watch over his mate solici-
tously. When her clutch of eggs numbered eight or ten,
she was usually ready to set. She kept to her nest for the
required number of thirty days except for brief periods to
get food and water. At hatching time, Aunt Het braved
Oscar's baleful hisses to remove the gosling to prevent
the babies from being mashed in the nest under the heavy
body of the old goose. They were returned to the care of
the parents when all had left the shell.

Maude and Oscar led their offspring over the fresh
grass encouraging them in soft tones to nibble tender
shoots of clover leaves. Majestic in stance, with his head
proudly lifted, Oscar surveyed the surroundings alert to
any hint of danger. A rooster or hen dare not approach for
he would lower his head, spread his white wings to an

awesome width, and charge hissing at the intruder. Domestic geese can fly, but they take to their wings only under extreme stress. Heavy from over-eating and not much exercise, Maude and Oscar were not inclined to fly. Occasionally I have seen them spread their wings and run squawking, barely skimming the ground when a horse galloped too close.

A gander can use his wings with telling effect, however, when angered or frightened. One spring I had had an unpleasant encounter with Oscar and stood in fear of him ever after. Charmed by the flock of yellow goslings with Maude and Oscar, I had approached to get better acquainted. In a flash the gander attacked. He nipped my legs with his sharp bill and beat me with his strong wings as I ran screaming for shelter. My thighs were soon black and blue with bruises and my legs covered with blood blisters and nip marks. Oscar won that confrontation, and I never came near his flock again when he was on duty. Possibly Aunt Het gave me the goslings that year so that I could enjoy them as pets, without fear of interference from the old gander.

When school started in the fall, I gave Jack and Jill scant attention. Off early in the morning to catch the school wagon and home late in the afternoon with chores to do, I seldom saw my pets. As days shortened I was pressed to get in wood, pick up chips to start morning fires, split lightwood, draw water to fill the tank on the old Majestic range, and get up eggs before dark.

One Saturday morning in December, when I stopped to open the door to Jack and Jill's coop, I found it empty. I had closed it the night before, assuming that the geese, who went to bed early, were inside. Alarmed, I sought my father who was harnessing the horses.

"Daddy, have you seen Jack and Jill?" My voice quivered as I spoke.

"No." His brown eye showed concern. "I can't remember seeing them yesterday or the day before either, come to think of it."

I ran back to the house to ask Mother about them and she came out to help. Together with Laddie at our heels, we began to search.

The barn—maybe they had been shut up in the grain barn—but they were not there. Calling loudly, I ran from place to place. At last, I turned to the long bean field behind the hay barn because I thought I had heard a faint cry. A movement at the far end caught my eye. I ran down the rows of bean stubble, gray and frosty in the early morning light, but saw nothing. Then the faint call again; at last I saw a flash of white. When I reached Jack, he was struggling to rise. He staggered a foot or two, uttered a mournful call, a poor imitation of his robust trumpet, then collapsed again, his long neck stretched on the frozen earth. I lifted him quickly, shocked to find his body so light.

"Where is Jill?" I asked stroking his dull feathers. I held the exhausted bird in my arms and began to search for his mate along the rail fence until I found her. Almost hidden in an angle of the fence, she appeared to be resting, but she was dead and probably had been for several days. She had died a natural death for her lovely white feathers were undisturbed.

By this time Mother and Laddie had caught up with me. She gently lifted Jill's body and slowly our little procession turned toward the house. Daddy met us halfway. He took the lifeless form saying he would bury it for me. The task of burying my pets had fallen to him often before, but he did it without complaint. On a farm both birth and death are commonplace realities, but I still suffered over the loss of each pet.

Mother and I entered the warm kitchen to minister to the needs of the living. I offered Jack his favorite, a biscuit, but he took no notice. He was too weak to eat. Exhausted by his ceaseless pacing and calling, he too was near death. Finally Mother mixed some corn meal and warm water, opened his bill, and forced some of the mixture down his throat. Placing him in a box near the stove, I sat by him stroking and talking to him. Several times during the day we repeated the feeding until he began to stir. By next day, he ate a little but would not leave the box. When I came near, he would lift his head, blink, and gently nibble my fingers. At last he began to talk to me in soft tones, and I knew he would recover.

It was a week before he was ready to return to his own world outside, but he was dependent on personal attention. Having lost Jill, he found a substitute of sorts in human companionship. Gradually, he adjusted and returned to his old routine. He slept alone in his coop under the walnut tree, but he usually stopped at the kitchen steps for a good night call. One of us would go with a biscuit for him; then he would enter his coop and allow us to close it for the night.

Jack lived for several years. A solitary figure roving the yard with dignified, measured pace, he appeared to be happy enough. He never took another mate though Aunt Het's geese were near enough for him to visit. Like a widower who has enjoyed a happy marriage, he found no one to take Jill's place.

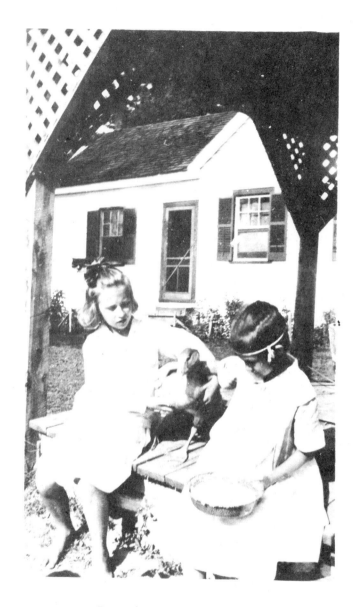

Louise and Ann with Jack

CHAPTER XVIII

Wild Game

"Until the middle of the 19th century hunting and fishing, like farming, were considered 'subsistence' activities, not only in Virginia but throughout most of North America. They were regarded generally as either necessary or at least helpful in maintaining an acceptable living standard." This statement appeared in 1975 in an article concerning the origins of conservation. It accurately reflects the attitude toward hunting in our community in 1915. Regulations in Virginia had been piecemeal during the first decade and a half of the century. Even these had been the result of pressure by sportsmen's publications and organizations to practice proper etiquette in the field and to develop an aesthetic appreciation for the game habitat. In 1916, the Department of Game and Inland Fisheries was established by Act of the General Assembly to require hunting licenses, establish hunting seasons, and employ game wardens.

Men in our neighborhood were law-abiding citizens who approved the game laws in principle, and who hunted mainly on their own property which they could do without a license. Enforcement of regulations was lax. The game warden seldom appeared, and most people went on much as they had before. However, my cousin Dick Walden considered himself a true sportsman. All his life he demonstrated a respect for wildlife and an appreciation for field and stream.

Dick learned to shoot at an early age. Every white family possessed a gun; the man of the family knew how to shoot it and trained his sons to use it as they grew up. A gun was needed to shoot hawks and crows, and an occasional predator in the chicken yard. If the hens were disturbed at night, the farmer went out with his gun and shot the intruder. It was a matter of pride among boys to learn to shoot well enough to take care of these situations when they arose and to be able to kill a few rabbits and squirrels, the first game that boys usually hunted. Some never developed much beyond this stage; others made hunting a lifetime pursuit, and Dick became one of these.

Uncle Rich was never a hunter. Dick loved to go into the woods with my father, and it is probable that he taught him to shoot.

"Where do you stand when John shoots the gun?" My mother once asked the five-year old boy.

"I get behind him and peep between his legs," he answered.

"Well, I guess you won't get shot if that's what you do," she replied, reassured that he was out of harm's way.

The woods became Dick's playground during hunting season. Early in the morning, before it was light, he slipped out to find a big oak or chestnut tree where the squirrels were cutting. Waiting patiently until he could get a good shot, he usually brought home two or three each morning. Skinned and cleaned, they made a welcome addition to the larder. It was the same with rabbits. In the afternoons after school, or on Saturdays if enough hours of daylight remained before barn chores, Dick and Sport, his beagle hound, would be off after rabbits which were equally acceptable as food.

Aunt Het was skilled in preparing game for the table, as most housewives were. She soaked the rabbits or squirrels in salted water to which vinegar had been added. The salt drew out the blood, the vinegar reduced the gamey flavor, and rendered the meat more palatable. Fried lightly, then steamed under a pan lid until tender, both squirrels and rabbits were greeted with pleasure by farm families.

As Dick grew older and developed into a crack shot, quail hunting became his favorite. He loved the solitude of the hunt, the walk through the quiet fields on a crisp fall day, the whirr of the birds as they rose in the air when a covey was flushed and their lovely calls to each other. "Bob-white, bob-white" and the answering whistle of the female were a joy to him. He could imitate each call when he wished, and enjoyed whistling "bob white" and waiting for the answer. Quail are small birds which present a rapidly moving target to the hunter. To raise the gun to shoulder, take aim, compensate for the speed of the flying bird and bring down a quail require skill, concentration, good eyesight, and marvelous control. Dick seldom came back empty-handed when he went hunting.

We all considered quail a real delicacy for the table. Troublesome to prepare, they were still worth it. The feathers had to be picked off dry, unlike chickens which were scalded. Birdshot had to be removed, and the little bird cleaned, soaked in salt water, and fried. Dick often shared his game with us, and birds for breakfast the morning after a hunt were a special treat.

Night hunting, an entirely different sport from daytime hunting, also became a favorite with Dick. He kept several coon dogs which had been trained to pick up the scent of an animal and trail it to a hollow ground or tree where it had taken refuge. Armed with his gun, and carrying a lantern and an axe, he followed his dogs to where they stood baying beneath a tree with the coon probably high above them in the branches. Getting it down required different methods. Sometimes, if the coon was in a hollow, he climbed the tree and killed it; if the tree was small he cut it down, but if he could get a good shot he killed it in the tree. If it fell to the ground and the near-frenzied dogs reached it first, the pelt would be torn and worthless. Aside from the sport, the trick was to bring home the animals in good condition. Raccoons were valued for their pelts, and fur buyers paid good money for a big hide.

Dick skinned the coons and stretched the hides on homemade stretchers, often nothing more than a three-foot length of hickory sapling which bent easily without breaking. It was bent nearly double and slipped inside the pelt. When released, the branches sprang apart making a tight fit for the hide. Some pelts were stretched on lengths of boards shaped to fit. When the hides had dried enough to stop shrinking, he removed the skins and nailed them to the side of the barn until he could sell them. His display was often impressive, but I hated to see the lifeless forms; somehow I was always on the side of the coons.

Raccoons are beautiful animals. A coon has thick grayish-brown fur, a handsome bushy ringed tail, and a keen muzzle. Its eyes are encircled with a black ring which gave rise to nicknames like the "masked bandit." One interesting characteristic of the raccoon is its propensity for washing its food. Its forepaws are remarkably like black human hands; tiny and dexterous, they hold its food for it to eat daintily and quickly. In spite of all this, coons were extremely unpopular with farmers. In summer, they invaded the cornfields when the ears were at milk stage, climbed the stalk, stripped back the shucks with those marvelous little hands, and gorged themselves on fresh corn. Perhaps they felt that, protected by shucks, the corn did not need washing. It was not unusual to find dozens of stalks broken and the ears ruined on the edge of a field on the morning after coons had visited it. Night animals, they were never seen in the day. By the end of the season coons could destroy a good part of a corn crop. Therefore, Dick's efforts to decrease the coon population were applauded by the neighborhood men.

Perhaps one reason I liked coons was the stories my mother told of her pet coon. When she was a small child, someone gave her a baby raccoon which she raised. It was clever and playful and made an amusing but mischievous pet. She said that it liked to play hide and seek. Someone would sit on the front steps, hold the coon, and wait until she had hidden. As soon as it was released it would scamper without fail to her hiding place. It roamed the house apparently, and loved her toothbrush which it could hold in its paws and nibble on. It also liked fresh milk. When Aunt Dicey would come from the cowpen in the evening carrying a pail of milk in each hand and one balanced on her head, Cooney would meet her, clamber up her dress to her shoulder and drink from the pail on her head. With both hands full she could do nothing but screech and berate "dat debblish coon." The milk from which he had drunk would be given to the hogs, a waste which the family deplored. Eventually Cooney disappeared, a victim of Aunt Dicey's vindictiveness, and Mother grieved for him for months. I always felt that as pets went, a coon must have been the epitome. I longed for a pony and a pet coon, neither of which desires was ever achieved.

Dick hunted opossums as well as raccoons if the dogs happened to scent one, but they were lesser quarry, the hides bringing little. The colored community received an opposum carcass with pleasure. It was an oily meat, but they cooked it with sweet potatoes and considered it a delicacy. Occasionally an opossum would raid the hen-house and cause such a ruckus that my father would hurry out in the middle of the night to quell the riot. If it could not escape, the 'possum played dead. It would lie inert so long that it oftened fooled its captors into believing it was really dead. Next morning the "dead body" would have walked off. "Playing 'possum" was a phrase in common use when someone feigned sleep or a faint. Other predators like foxes or weasels had to be killed on the spot if they could be caught; 'possums were slow-moving and easily captured. "Playing 'possum" was a good defense mechanism for them.

Fox hunting attracted men who had horses and loved the chase of several miles behind hounds on a frosty morning. A carry-over from the time when it was a "gentleman's sport" and only landowners with saddle horses and leisure time could enjoy it, it attracted only a select few. They kept fox hounds, a special breed, for the chase. These were handsome black dogs with a touch of brown about the eyes and ears; they gave a piercing cry when in pursuit that could be heard for miles. Men who loved the sport have been known to take the horse from the plow, throw on a saddle, and join the hunt when they heard the hounds baying in the distance.

Fox pelts were valuable for sale, but often they were ruined by the dogs before they could be retrieved. The brush or fox tail was awarded to the owner of the dog which led the pack to the kill. A fox fur properly tanned and fitted with clasps was a prized neckpiece. Dick gave me one once when I was in college, and I flaunted it proudly. Mink, of course, were more desirable than fox furs.

Wild turkeys were fairly common in this decade and turkey hunting was a popular sport. The hunter wanted to be in the woods before dawn when the turkeys were just coming from the roost or late in the afternoon when they were going to roost. Hunters usually had already located a roosting site easily identified by the droppings on the ground beneath. As the birds began to stir and leave the trees, the hunter would attempt to attract one away from the flock with a turkey caller. Fashioned from a small piece of wood, it could be made to sound like the gobbler or the hen depending on the skill of the caller. To bag a turkey was a triumph and good for many a story afterwards.

"I was crouched behind this big log over on the crest of the hill that makes up from the Exol; my legs had gone to sleep and I was near frozen—'twas really nippy that morning, when I heard this here scratching in the dry leaves, not mor'n ten feet away, look like to me. 'That's a turkey' I says to myself. 'Now if 'twill just move this way and git out in the open.' " The story teller would multiply the details: how he waited, didn't hear it no more, got out his caller, gave a few yelps, heard the rustling again. "There she was all of a sudden, a nice hen too close to shoot, I'd of blowed her all to pieces. I was raising my gun though when she flew—right over me. I turned, got her in my sights and fired. She fell in them little pines over to the left. I knew I had her but it took me a while to find her. When I got home the old lady was mad as thunder—cows waiting to be milked, you know—but when she saw that turkey, she clumb down off her high horse, I tell you. Bird weighed near ten pounds dressed—she's young and tender. Good eating." Turkey hunting brought out the raconteur in a man.

One year a couple of days before Thanksgiving my father, on a sudden impulse, decided to go hunting.

"Believe I'll slip down the woods and get us a turkey," he told my mother. "I saw where they've been roosting off from the back field. Should be coming in about now. Connie is going to knock off early and feed and milk for me." His eyes were shining in anticipation.

He didn't take off from work very often, but the boy in him demanded some recreation now and then.

"Go on. Bring me a turkey for Thanksgiving." Mother laughed gaily thinking, no doubt, that there was small chance of such luck. It was almost dark when he returned, but he was carrying a big gobbler and was full of all the details of the hunt. Thanksgiving was special that year because usually we did not have turkey except for Christmas.

About 1915, we began what became an annual event for the next ten years. We provided accommodations for a group of Baltimore businessmen who wanted a week's quail shooting. The birds were abundant in King and Queen then. Their natural habitat had not been disturbed by new farming practices which later would lead to their decline in numbers. The zigzag rail fences with blackberry vines, weeds, and bushes growing luxuriantly in their corners, offered excellent breeding places as well as a food supply. The tight wire fences which replaced the rail fences destroyed nesting sites and often proved to be death traps to birds caught in the meshes. A 1923 survey, however, of quail killed in Virginia by counties showed over 3,000 bagged in King and Queen for that year. Eight or ten years earlier they were probably even more plentiful. Our isolated community was a good choice for bird hunters.

On their first trip, the men came to Bowlers Wharf on the Baltimore steamboat. My father met them in the surrey with Connie following with the wagon to bring back their luggage and hunting gear. Mr. Musselman and Mr. Harriman, with two others whose names I have forgotten, made up the party. In succeeding years the foursome varied, but Mr. Harriman and Mr. Musselman were always among them. Mr. Musselman was a jovial, rotund little man whom his pals called "Fats." They joked with him constantly about his weight, his appetite, his stamina, and his shooting ability, all of which he accepted with good humor. He was my favorite, because he always brought me a present, usually books after he found out I liked to read. These became treasured volumes, some of which I have now. They provided a glimpse into his world of affluence, so unlike ours.

The men brought their guns and shells but my father secured some local men to serve as guides and to supply hunting dogs. Dick Walden and Cell Young, a knowledgeable woodsman, usually looked forward to their coming for they paid well. Each morning, soon after sun-up, they set off by twos, to be gone all day, each carrying a lunch, which Mother had packed. The men returned in late afternoon in high good humor if the hunting had been good, and it usually was. They were good shots, possessed excellent guns, and knew the techniques of hunting.

Mr. Harriman directed the disposal of the game. They gutted the birds, strung them on a cord, and hung them on the porch too high to be reached by cats or dogs. This was the only refrigeration which we could provide, but in late November or early December it was all that was needed. They took the birds back to Baltimore with them ostensibly to be used on their tables. Probably it was to have proof positive of their successful hunting trip. If they had happened to shoot a rabbit on the way home, they gave it to Connie, who received it gladly.

The four slept in our big upstairs bedroom with the two double beds. Auntie and I occupied the "little room," the small, unheated room over the wide central hall, for the duration. There was a wood-burning heater in the room which they fired up when they had taken care of the game. They cleaned up a little and rested until called to dinner.

All day my mother and Maria Dell, hired for the week, had been busy preparing the sumptuous meal. To cook a big breakfast and put up four lunches, they had risen at 5:00 a.m., but the real work of the day was dinner. The men were naturally hearty eaters, and after tramping the fields all day, they were ready to do justice to the meal. The picture of the table is clear before me. The bright lamp light reveals the big ham, my father's specialty, before his place. Before my mother's were the coffee pot and cups, and spread between them bowls heaped with mashed potatoes, turnip greens, and stewed tomatoes. There were dishes of spiced peaches, pear preserves, and rich country butter. Over it all, floated the tantalizing odor of freshly baked rolls. As the men ate, there were jokes and teasing, plates were refilled, and compliments came thick and fast. "Best ham in the country. Did you ever eat better, Fats?"

"Never did, Gaylord, never did. Pass the rolls, please. You can't have them all." Dessert was never refused. Mother's lemon pie and cherry dumplings were favorites.

Many evenings, the men gathered in the living room to smoke a pipe and talk. Gaylord Harriman would be prevailed upon to sing. Often in demand as a soloist at funerals, he said, he sang hymns which we all knew. With Mother at the piano, his rich voice would fill the room with "Lead, Kindly Light," or "Abide with Me," two of my favorites to this day.

They paid $100 for the week, a sum which seemed enormous to us. Most of the food was home grown, oysters cost twenty-five cents a quart, and labor was still cheap. We looked forward, with pleasure, to the week the huntsmen, as we called them, came because it brought us a breath of the outside world and some ready money as well. After a year or two, they drove down in a big touring car which caused a stir in the neighborhood. If they were not really wealthy men, they seemed so to us who were impressed by their handsome guns, their hunting coats and their high top, laced walking shoes. To men who possessed only gum boots or everyday shoes and a ragged coat for hunting, they were gorgeously outfitted. As the men grew older their hunts started later in the morning and ended earlier in the afternoon. I think they continued to come the last year or two out of friendship and love of my mother's cooking, as much as the love of hunting.

Fur-bearing game provided a lucrative source of income for some men during cold weather. Marsh land along the Dragon and its tributary, Exol, was teeming with muskrats and some mink and otter. Beaver were unkown along the stream then. Trapping, another form of hunting, is not a convivial sport. It was done in solitude by men who did not mind the cold and wet or walking long distances.

Trappers had to know the habits of the wild animals, the places they frequented, and their food; they had to be keenly observant and to possess a sense of responsibility. No one admired the trapper who did not visit his traps regularly to release the captured animals. At best trapping involves an element of cruelty, but the responsible person was careful to set his traps along waterways where the animal would drown after being caught. This, however, did not always happen. Trappers told of animals which had gnawed off a foot and escaped leaving the proof in the trap.

Hunting and trapping served the purpose of keeping the game population in balance as well as providing its many benefits to those who practiced it.

CHAPTER XIX

World War I

When the United States declared war on Germany, April 5, 1917, I was at home on the farm, Rising farm prices and contributions to Belgian Relief had been in progress for some time. No new effects on the farm were felt immediately. Plowing, planting, cultivating, and harvesting proceeded on schedule as our country geared up for war. In September, however, I began school in Urbanna, leaving home for the first time to enter a whole new world. Amid all the changes in my personal life, to which I was struggling to adjust, I soon became aware of the atmosphere of excitement and patriotism pervading the town.

War posters appeared in store windows, in the bank, and the post offices. Uncle Sam, with his pointing finger saying I WANT YOU for U.S. ARMY, fascinated me. Another poster showed a beautiful lady above a caption about Victory Liberty Loans. There were local men, both in Urbanna and back in King and Queen County, who answered Uncle Sam's call, but as a ten-year old I hardly noticed. At home, my father and mother were much more concerned, I'm sure. Brantley and Alvah, my father's two youngest brothers, joined the army and were sent overseas. I realize now what a time of anxiety this was for them, but I was not really conscious of what war meant. I remember thinking of the Kaiser as the cause of it all, and planning terrible things that I would do to him if I had the chance.

Ladies in Urbanna, like patriotic women everywhere, began to knit for the soldiers. Even the children took part, and I acquired a little knitting bag, some yarn, and a pair of needles. I knitted wristlets, the simplest item I could possibly have tried. I felt that I was contributing to the popular war effort, but I don't recall any of my wristlets being sent overseas.

I remember the music of the period more clearly. People were singing the catchy war tunes: "Tipperary," "Keep the Home Fires Burning," "The Long, Long Trail" and the amusing "Madamoiselle from Arementieres." Others were "K-K-K-Katy, Beautiful Katy," the stammering song that was parodied into "K-K-K-K.P.," and the bugle song:

> "I can't get'em up,
> I can't get'em up,
> I can't get'em up in the morning ..."

During the summer of 1917 and 1918, when Martha was home from college, she played these songs over and over. Marguerite and I loved to lie on our stomachs on their parlor floor on hot days and listen. We learned most of the words and sang along, I with my usual disregard for tune or discords. Marguerite, more musically talented than I as well as two years older, could play some of the songs herself, to my undisguised envy and admiration. Snatches of these songs still come back to me especially:

> "There's long long trail a-winding,
> Into the land of my dreams
> Where the nightingales are singing
> And the white moon beams"

As the war advanced and before our country's entry, an important part of America's war effort was supplying food for the allies. The need for fats, sugar, and foodstuffs was acute. Herbert Hoover, at first as head of Belgian

Relief, and later as Food Administrator, launched a tremendous campaign to conserve food. "Hooverizing" was a term coined to mean any of a multitude of small measures practiced by housewives to avoid waste: serving smaller portions, cleaning food from cooking pans and serving dishes, using more corn bread, observing meatless days and wheatless days, using syrup instead of sugar, and cutting back on the use of pork. Aunt Het used to refer to her forefinger as her Hoover finger because she used it to wipe the last clinging drops of albumin from an egg shell. Eggs were bringing the fantastic price of 60 cents a dozen, and we made them go as far as we could.

Young people in Urbanna adopted a few army styles and some new expressions. We thought the army trench caps were becoming and perched one on our curls, if we could find one. My closest chum in Urbanna often wore a khaki army shirt, an older brother's cast-off, in place of a sweater, and I yearned for one to replace the hand-knit sweaters which I had to wear. We talked about doughboys, K.P., and U-boats. "Doing your bit" became a common phrase and "slacker," a person who was not doing his bit for the war effort, was an almost slanderous epithet. I still find myself saying, sometimes, "I don't want to be a slacker."

The Great Influenza Epidemic of 1918 is the thing I remember best. The outbreak was subsiding in our area by the signing of the armistice, but it already had taken a terrible toll and affected communities statewide. According to statistics from the Virginia State Board of Health, nearly 8,000 died of flu before the epidemic ended. National figures are placed between 400,000 and 500,000 deaths.

In our area people were falling ill everywhere, and the fear of contagion had reached the level of terror. Public gatherings of all kinds were canceled, schools closed, churches did not hold services, and people kept to themselves as much as possible, In October, as the epidemic spread, the Urbanna school closed and my parents brought me home.

I was playing outdoors late one afternoon when I began to have a severe chill. In the house, Mother put her hand on my head to find me burning with fever. Consternation took hold of the family. It was almost night and my parents realized that getting a doctor before the next day was virtually impossible. I was put to bed upstairs in the bedroom where Auntie and I slept, but everyone knew there was nothing to be done. My temperature was high, but as no one had a thermometer, they could only guess. My head hurt and I was extremely restless. The family went to bed telling themselves that my illness might not be "flu" but knowing instinctively that it was.

Next morning I was no better, and my father rode horseback to Center Cross for Dr. DeShazo. He found him bleary-eyed and exhausted after having been in his buggy 16 hours the previous day, visiting the sick and dying.

"John, is her temperature very high?" the doctor asked.

"She's mighty hot," my father replied cautiously.

"I'll send this medicine by you, and try to see her tomorrow. I have a patient at Upright who is desperately ill. I have to go there now, but I'll try to see her as soon as I can. You know that, don't you?"

"Yes, doctor. We'll expect you when you can." There were only two doctors within a radius of fifteen miles. Dr. Brooksie, who had set my broken arm, and Dr. DeShazo were both driving themselves to the point of physical exhaustion day and night. How long could they stand up under the relentless pressure was worrying all those who depended on them.

That afternoon Auntie began to complain of a headache, and by suppertime she was in bed. With two sick my parents were truly alarmed. What if the whole family succumbed! Virulent and highly contagious, influenza had swept through whole families often taking the life of at least one. If we all go down, what will we do, they wonderd.

The question was soon answered. My father was too sick to get up on the second day, but Mother went to the kitchen to prepare breakfast for herself and Willie Temple, who was our live-in help at the time. Willie had made the fire in the cook stove and gone to the barn to milk before she appeared. When he returned, he stopped on the kitchen porch.

"Miss Kate, I'se leaving de milk out her. I'se scared to come in. Could you put my breffus out here, please m'am?" he called.

"All right, Willie. I don't want you to get sick too. I'll fix a plate and leave it out there." she answered.

In a few minutes, Uncle Richie appeared in the yard and spoke to Mother from a distance.

"We heard from Martha last night. She telephoned to Center Cross, and they sent the message by Lieper Tuppence. The college has closed, and she's coming to West Point on the train. I'm hitching the horse up to go to meet her now," he called.

"She's not sick, is she? Lord knows, I hope not. Is Settie all right?" (Mother years ago had shortened the name Sister Hettie and slurred it to become one word, Settie.)

"Yes, so far. I'm not coming in. Where's John?"

"He's sick now. I'm the only one up," and she began to cry.

As the day wore on Mother ran from the bedroom to the kitchen repeatedly. She was at her best in illness; nothing was too much trouble, if it relieved the discomfort of the sick one. She rubbed my father's aching back, brought Auntie chilled grape juice which she had canned in the summer, made me some chicken soup, and all day she prayed that the doctor would come.

"Just let him get here, please, Lord," she begged. "Send us some help." Over and over as she kept up her ceaseless ministering she repeated her prayer. At last, as the sun sank toward the horizon she heard the sound of a buggy stopping at the gate. Dr. DeShazo wearily climbed the stairs, took our temperatures, and counted out a supply of pills to leave for us.

"Lots of people are worse off than they are, Kate," he told her as he prepared to leave. "If they don't get pneumonia, I think they'll pull through. Now don't wear yourself out looking after them. The disease has to run its course, you know. Try not to get it yourself. I won't get back over here again right away."

Somewhat reassured, Mother prepared for bed, but before midnight she was stricken too. The sudden onslaught of the disease was one of its characteristics. By morning, she was too ill to rise.

When Willie came from the barn with the milk, and no one had come to the kitchen to prepare breakfast, he realized that the entire family was ill. Visibly upset, he found Uncle Richie at his barn and told him the situation.

"Willie, can't you strain the milk and put it away? You've seen Miss Kate do it often enough. Feed the pigs and chickens; then come down to my house and we'll give you some breakfast."

"Yes suh, I kin do dat, but afterwards I gwine home," the frightened boy answered.

"If you do that, who will take care of the barn work? I can't do my work and Mr. Eubank's too, and the sick folks have to have a fire. We need you to keep wood in the house. You won't get flu if you don't go where they are." To Willie's credit, his sense of responsibility and loyalty overcame his fear, and he returned to the house.

Uncle Rich went home to breakfast with the dreaded news that John, Kate, Sister, and Louise were all ill. Our lives were probably saved because Martha, who had come home from college the day before, risked her own life to come to our aid.

The students at Westhampton College, where Martha was then a sophomore, were being housed temporarily downtown because in the spring of 1918 the United States government had contracted to rent the entire University of Richmond campus and had turned it into a hospital. The risk of contagion being seen as greater in the city, the girls were sent home during the worst of the flu epidemic though the young men at Richmond College remained on campus.

Young, healthy, and even then planning to give her life to full-time Christian service, Martha, in defiance of danger, came forward to nurse us. Aunt Het prepared food, but until our fevers abated, little was needed. Willie brought wood to the second floor and left it at the head of the stairs, and Martha administered the medicine, kept up the fires, and attended to our personal needs. Miraculously both she and Willie remained well.

One by one we recovered. Weakened and shaky, my father ventured to the barn to help Willie, and Mother crept to the kitchen to do the cooking. Auntie and I, who had had more severe attacks, took longer to recuperate, but not everyone in the community was so fortunate. The outbreak declined after a month. Life gradually returned to normal, Martha went back to college, and I reentered school in Urbanna.

The epidemic had, of course, reached greater heights in Richmond. As we began to recover, Martha described the situation as it was when she had left to come home.

"The streets of Richmond were completely deserted as the streetcar passed through them on the way to Main Street Station," she told us. "As I looked out not a person could be seen. Some stray bits of paper blowing in the wind were the only movement up and down the street. At the station there were no porters to help with my baggage and several ticket windows were empty. The whistle of the approaching train was the most mournful sound I think I ever heard."

"Were many people on the train?" asked Auntie.

"No, only a few, and they huddled to themselves afraid to make contact with anyone."

A friend later described the death of her uncle, a student at Medical College of Virginia. His body was sent home by train in a sealed casket which was not brought into the house when it reached home, but was left outside overnight until the burial next day. In cities, mass graves were a necessity to cope with the numerous deaths. The army camps with their crowded conditions saw the highest death toll. Fortunately the war came to an end soon after the epidemic began to subside.

The dramatic silencing of the guns in Europe at the eleventh hour of the eleventh day of the eleventh month thrilled the world and continued to do so long afterwards, as Armistice Day was commemorated annually. The duration of our country's involvement in the war had been short, but it brought tremendous changes in its aftermath. Our way of life, so slow to change over the previous decades, lurched suddenly into the twentieth century. People who could not adapt to change withdrew into private lives isolating themselves more and more from the world around them. Others threw off the shackles of the past and plunged into the new life welcoming it with exhilaration.

CHAPTER XX

Making Molasses

"When will the sorghum be ready to cut, John?" my mother asked at breakfast one day in early October.

"It will be another week or two, I guess," my father answered. "The heads haven't begun to change color yet."

"Have you found anyone to make the molasses?"

"That's just the problem. Josh Holmes' equipment is so old I don't want to get him again. Last year the boiler pan had rust spots on it and that makes a dark colored syrup. I like it bright. I think I'll see if I can get Jim Croxton from Center Cross. He ground for Pete Richardson last year, and the molasses was excellent."

"Will he bring his mill this far?" Aunt Gay inquired.

"Oh, I think so if I can get a few other seats. I'll see what Cell Young and Miskell Dyle plan to do. Of course, Brother Richie will bring his cane here and we'll divide the expenses."

I listened with interest. I thought it was fascinating to see the grinding of the cane and watch the horse on his endless journey round and round the mill. Although my sympathy for the horse was aroused, I did not waste much thought on him. I was too pleased at the prospect of a day which provided some excitement. Not as big a day as wheat threshing, it was still something to look forward to. I poured some molasses on a buttered biscuit, ate it with enjoyment, and listened as the conversation continued.

"Maybe you'll have a few gallons to sell this year if the yield is good," suggested Aunt Gay.

"Maybe. I hope so," replied my father, never one to encourage false hopes.

I slipped out to the field after dinner where the sorghum grew tall and thick. By this time of year it stood 10 to 12 feet high with heavy clusters of seeds at the top of the long, slender stalks. I loved to walk between the rows and listen to the whispering of the leaf blades stirred by the breeze. As it ripened the seed clusters turned dark red forming thick bunches which attracted black birds and crows. It was a beautiful crop with its rich green leaves, red seeds, and dense growth.

The seeds had been planted in May or early June in hills about a foot apart down the long rows. After the seeds germinated, the plants were thinned to four or five in a hill. The cane looked much like corn at first with long slender blades of green appearing at intervals up the stalk though it was planted thicker than corn and did not require as much tending. Cane was grown for the juice which came from the stalks when crushed. The leaves did not provide fodder for animals, though the seeds could be mixed with other grains for poultry feed.

Sorghum was harvested just before frost, because cold made the leaves tough and harder to strip from the stalks. It was not cut until a day or two before the grinding took place, because the juice might sour and ruin.

I came home one afternoon to find Jim Croxton and my father setting up the mill for an early start next morning. Nearby the evaporator (boiler) stood with a supply of wood stacked and ready to keep a fire burning when needed. Charles and Connie were in the cane field stripping the leaves from the stalks. They had cut down several rows of cane, chopped off the seed heads and loaded the stalks on a wagon which would be hauled to the mill next morning.

"Oh, Daddy, tomorrow is Friday and I have to go to school. I'll miss everything," I cried. "Can't I stay home just one day?"

"Of course not, Louise, but you won't miss out entirely. We won't finish until some time Saturday. Marguerite is coming home for the weekend so both of you can enjoy the fun," he replied.

I was delighted. I had not seen Marguerite since school started because we attended different schools, and I was eager to hear what she had been doing. Friday afternoon when I returned from school, I found a big batch of molasses had already been made, but Uncle Richie's cane would be ground next day, and we could watch the entire proceedings.

The mill consisted of three rollers. It was operated by a horse hitched to a long pole, or sweep, which turned the rollers as the horse plodded around the mill in a circle. The cane stalks were fed into one side of the mill and crushed between the rollers. The crushed stalks soon formed a big pile which had to be moved away and spread to dry. It could be used later as bedding in the cowpen, but if left in a pile, the damp, shredded stalks would sour and give off a foul odor.

A bright green juice ran from the crushed stalks. It was strained through several layers of cloth as it ran into a barrel. When enough juice had been collected to make a batch of molasses, the cooking began. The boiler, or evaporator, was an open, shallow galvanized pan about 4 x 8 feet and 6 inches in depth. It had several partitions along its length, so that as the syrup cooked, it could be moved along into sections of the boiler where it cooked more slowly. A fire was built under the pan and kept burning during the process.

As soon as the fresh, watery juice began to boil, a dark foam appeared on top. This had to be skimmed off with a hand made strainer. Some people used a piece of copper with holes punched into it attached to a long handle. Others simply used a piece of wire tacked to a broom handle. The stirring, cooking, and skimming went on for three or four hours with a man constantly in attendance to keep the fire burning and to see that the syrup did not burn as it thickened. Then it became more important to control the heat because too hot a fire might scorch the syrup, or over-cook it. To do this the tender would add small amounts of wood to the fire using a hard wood that burned slowly. At last, the man cooking the molasses would begin to sample it to determine when it had reached the right consistency. If not cooked enough, the syrup would be thin and "runny."

Marguerite and I had been frolicking around the mill and boiler all morning. We enjoyed the crisp fall air, the smell of the wood smoke from the fire, and its comforting warmth as the day became colder. Now as the first batch neared completion we stood ready, each with a wooden paddle to sample the hot syrup.

"Be careful, Marguerite, that stuff is hot," her father warned. "Don't let any drip on your hand or you'll get a blister. Cool it before you taste it."

"Mine's cool enough now. Gee, it's good," I cried as I touched my tongue to the warm syrup on the paddle.

"I don't think it's ready yet," my uncle said. "Louise, run to the house and get me a dish. I want to send Het a sample to see if she thinks it's too thin."

I ran off for the dish and Uncle Rich poured a spoonful or two into it. "Now take it to your mother and let me know what she says," he instructed Marguerite.

The molasses bubbled in the pan, but no wood was added to the fire until Marguerite returned.

"It's done," she shouted as she trotted up. "If it's any thicker you won't be able to pour it from the jug next winter, Mama says," and she laughed in delight at the prospect.

The syrup thickened as it cooled; if it was thick when hot, in winter it would become almost semi-solid. "Slow as cold molasses in the wintertime" was a homely comparison understood by everybody who had ever waited for the syrup to pour from the barrel or from a molasses pitcher on a cold morning.

The big pan was tilted enough to drain the molasses into a lard tin covered with a strainer cloth. Thick, amber, and shining, the syrup smelled delicious, I thought. A new batch of juice was poured into the pan and the cooking began again.

When the last wagon load of cane had been ground, the horse was unhitched from the sweep and turned into the pasture for a well-earned rest. The mill-owner began to clean the mill and prepare it for loading on his wagon while the last of the juice bubbled in the boiler. Uncle Rich stood by watching this batch carefully to be sure that it did not over cook. Marguerite and I dipped our little paddles into the juice between fetching wood to keep the fire burning and chasing each other around the barn. Prince, untied for the day, romped with us. It was a carefree, happy time.

After the syrup had been strained into tins and the fire doused with water, the boiler pan was taken to the well, thoroughly washed, and loaded on the waiting wagon. With his equipment in order, Mr. Croxton was ready to talk business.

"I git every fourth gallon as my toll," he told my father. "How many did ya git? Twenty? Well you owes me five gallons."

"This tin has four gallons in it. I'll fill these two half-gallon jars and that will give you five. That's right, isn't it?" answered my father.

"Fine. Fine." He turned to Uncle Rich. "Now, Mr. Walden, how many gallons did ya' make?"

"Twenty-two," replied my uncle.

"Let's see, that's five 'n a half for me, ain't it?"

The toll received, the mill owner drove off to reach Cell Young's place a few miles away and go through the molasses-making process there the next week.

At our house, the crushed stalks and seed heads were cleared away and the newly made molasses carried to the smoke house for storage. Fifteen gallons should last us until next year, for it was an important part of the diet, and we did not want to run out.

The molasses pitcher was put on the table for each meal along with the butter, sugar, and cream. Breakfast usually ended with one or two hot biscuits and molasses. If dessert was not a part of other meals, molasses and bread added the sweet course which nearly everyone desired. Molasses also made a delicious gingerbread or molasses pudding. Served warm with a lemon sauce, it was a company dessert; cold with a glass of buttermilk, it was a wonderful after-school snack.

Molasses was the main ingredient for a candy-pulling, once a popular social event for young people. Molasses would be cooked down to a very thick syrup, then poured into a buttered dish or pan. When it was cool enough to handle, the mass was rolled into a ball and pulled out into a heavy rope. A boy and girl, with buttered hands to keep the candy from sticking, would pull it back and forth, stretching it out as far as it would go. In five or ten minutes the candy would change color to a rich golden shade. When it became too hard to pull it was laid out in a long piece to cool completely. It could then be cracked into bite-sized pieces. Another method was to cut the still pliable string with scissors into neat pieces.

The candy was good, but the fun lay in the pulling. A novice might have great difficulty with the sticky mass, and competition between couples to see who could pull the longest strands or make the neatest finished candy was keen.

By the time I was a teen-ager, more sophisticated entertainment had taken the place of candy pulling, but as a small child I watched older boys and girls having a good time with the long ropes of molasses taffy.

Home made molasses has virtually disappeared in our area. Few farmer's would bother with the small crop needed for one-family consumption today. Where sorghum is grown the crop is cultivated on a larger scale and milling has undergone many refinements. Gone is the horse operated mill and the drama from the operation.

CHAPTER XXI

Aunt Gay's Death

Aunt Gay was in failing health when she retired from teaching, but I did not realize it. She seemed much the same to me: reading, helping with the housework, crocheting, attending church regularly, and always ready to play parchesi or flinch with me. However, one weekend I came home to find mother in a highly emotional state.

"Sister is ill," she told me. "We took her to the doctor Tuesday, and he has put her on some very powerful medicine. It's her heart." She broke down and sobbed as she gave me the details. Apparently Auntie had had a mild angina attack, but to my mother the situation was devastating.

"She has to take one drop of the medicine three times a day. The doctor says two drops might kill her, and three drops would certainly be fatal."

We were all impressed with the precarious condition of Aunt Gay's health. She was not to climb stairs more than once a day, she must rest a great deal, and she must take the medicine without fail. The only dietary restriction was in eating hog meat. Always a hearty eater, Auntie had for years led a sedentary life. The combination of rich food and little exercise had produced not only heart trouble but kidney and liver trouble, as we found out later. She was more seriously ill than my father or I suspected, but to my mother, who lived in a perpetual state of anxiety lest disaster strike one of her loved ones, her death was imminent. She suffered the pangs of grief long before the final hour arrived.

Administering the drop of medicine was a major concern and never done without an observer.

"I'm going to fix Auntie's medicine now. Come and watch to see that I put only one drop," she would call, and I would run to her and stare unblinkingly as she held the medicine dropper poised above the glass. If no one else was available, Auntie herself would be pressed into service. It would be difficult to estimate the number of doses thrown out because we were not positive that only one drop had fallen into the glass. A liquid form of nitroglycerin, the medicine was both odorless and colorless and left no trace after it had mixed with water.

On one occasion Auntie took a dose containing two drops. Mother had prepared the before-bedtime dose and left it for a minute. Auntie walked by, saw the glass of water, and thinking that she could save Mother some trouble, put in the drop, and drank the potion. When the mistake was discovered, consternation overcame us all. We had no idea what reaction two drops would produce. Would it be violent or quiet? Gradual or sudden? We could not telephone the doctor to ask for an antidote; a trip to his home and back would take two hours at least. The overdose would have done its work before then. There was nothing to do but wait.

I remember the night well. Mother declared she would sit up with Sister. Horror-struck as she was, sleep was unthinkable. Aunt Gay took the matter calmly and tried to reassure my mother.

"It's not your fault, Kate. It was a mistake. If my time has come, it is God's will and I accept it. Go to bed and get some rest, please."

"No, Sister. I should have brought the medicine to you. I'm to blame," and she wept inconsolably.

The night was long. As no ill-effects appeared, we relaxed somewhat. My father went to bed, I curled up on the foot of Auntie's bed and fell asleep and eventually she did too, but Mother sat upright in her chair by the bed. The lamp burned low, the stars faded, and the faint crowing of the rooster came with the first streaks of dawn, only then did Mother relax. Feeling the danger was over, she went to the kitchen, kindled the fire, and put on the coffee pot. Sending fervent thanks to God for his mercy, she prepared breakfast. Aunt Gay slept late that morning, but when Mother took up a breakfast tray, she ate heartily, apparently none the worse for the experience.

A year later Auntie suffered a fractured hip. Apparently the bone gave way under her weight as she was descending the stairs; the fall was the result rather than the cause of the fracture.

"Miss Gay, I'm going to have to send you to the hospital in Richmond." Dr. DeShazo announced after examining her. "But we will have to make special arrangements to move you. I'm going to see if I can get Marks from Tappahannock to take you." At this time there was no such thing as an ambulance; the nearest thing was the undertaker's new motorized hearse which had been utilized in a few cases. Fractures were usually put in splints at home after the bone had been set and left to heal. A hip was a more difficult problem. Marks, the undertaker, would help if he did not have a funeral to handle. This suggestion, however, did not go over well with either my mother or Aunt Gay.

"A hearse! No, indeed!" my mother exclaimed wildly. The very thought was horrifying.

"No, doctor. No hospital," Auntie replied calmly. "I haven't long to live, and I want to die at home." The sisters were united in their decision; they were not reluctant; they were adamant.

Faced with such an attitude, Dr. DeShazo yielded. He knew that his patients seldom entered a hospital except in the final extremity, and they did not usually live to come home. The word hospital was the equivalent of a death sentence to them.

Together Dr. DeShazo and my father contrived a kind of support for Auntie's leg. It was a light wooden frame, elevated under the knee, and padded with cotton. It resembled a kind of trough in which the leg lay for weeks until after a time the fracture healed. Eventually my aunt began to walk again with the aid of a crutch, but she was never able to do more than hobble about the house. She was not completely housebound for she attended church with the family once or twice, but the effort was too great, and Mother soon discouraged it.

By the next summer, Aunt Gay's condition had grown worse and she was confined to her bed. My mother was happy when school closed for the session, and I could help with the many trips up and down stairs to Auntie's room as well as with household tasks. The presence of hired help in the kitchen relieved my mother to some degree, but she was constantly in attendance at the bedside. As Auntie's condition deteriorated, she needed attention night and day. Neighbors and relatives took turns "sitting up" with her. Aunt Het, Clara Dyke, Mrs. Bennett, and Mrs. Moore, our nearest neighbors, came regularly. Farm women who had been up since daybreak working in their own homes did not hesitate to come to our aid and seemed glad to render such a service, but it could not go on. At last, Dr. DeShazo secured a trained nurse who moved into the house and took over the nursing for the last four weeks. Until the end came, she was on call at night if we needed her.

Embalming was not a general practice at this time. Aunt Gay's body was prepared for burial by the same kind people who had stood by us throughout her long illness. The undertaker brought the coffin, and her body remained at home until the day of the funeral. I remember helping my mother gather cabbage roses from the yard to lay on the casket. Auntie had loved flowers, and it seemed appropriate that those roses which she had tended and loved should be with her at the end. Bought flowers were rarely seen in the country; florists belonged to the city.

Aunt Gay's funeral was held the customary three days after her death. A prolonged rainy spell had preceded the day, but the sun shone brightly as the long procession drove the six miles from our home to the church where she had been a member since childhood. The churchyard was filled with buggies, surreys, and a few cars; many had come to pay their last respects to Miss Gay. There were relatives, friends, neighbors, and former pupils as well as members of the black community who had known and respected her. The funeral was conducted by the pastor who paid tribute to her years of service in both church and community, and the pastor's wife sang an interminable solo which I could never bear to hear afterwards. Her body joined that of her father and mother in the church cemetery.

At home we felt the loss keenly for many months. It was my first encounter with death close at hand—the first break in the immediate family circle. Aunt Gay had been a ready resource for information. "Auntie's a walking dictionary," a young nephew once said, and it is true, we turned to her for answers frequently. I had admired her intellectual attainments and her dignity, but beyond that she had always been my champion and my mentor. I had truly loved her and I missed her sorely.

For my mother the loss was even more devastating. Possessing an exceptionally loving nature, she had nursed her sister with untiring devotion during her illness, and though at the point of physical exhaustion, she found it hard to accept her death. The close tie which had united them through the years could not be severed easily.

The three of us took up our round of daily activities once more, but we continued to grieve in silence.

CHAPTER XXII

The Dragon

"Lewisville" is located in the fork of the Dragon and its tributary, Exol. The Dragon, a fresh water stream, rises in Essex County not far from the King and Queen community of Powcan and writhes its way eastward to form the boundary between King and Queen and Essex Counties along its upper length and Gloucester and Middlesex Counties lower down. About fifteen miles from its mouth, the stream widens to form Meggs Bay and becomes the Piankatank, a beautiful, unpolluted tidal river, which empties into the Chesapeake Bay.

Formed at least a million years ago when the waters of the Pleistocene Ocean receded and the Coastal Plain emerged, Dragon Run, as it is sometimes called, contains remains of marine beds and fossil shells. Marl beds with shell fragments are common along exposed banks of the stream.

This apparently sluggish stream is insignificant in appearance in comparison with the mighty Rappahannock River just a few miles away. Several exceptional features, however, make the Dragon unique. First, it contains rare specimens of plant and animal life and is noted for its growth of cypress trees, seldom found this far north. Trees growing along the borders give its waters their characteristic brown stain from the tannic acid found in the bark. Sailing vessels coming up the Piankatank to Freeport to be loaded with lumber are said to have filled their water barrels from the Dragon because the tannic acid gave the water medicinal value and made it keep better than spring water on long voyages. Stands of loblolly and shortleaf pine were once abundant, but today only a few specimens of old growth remain on cut-over areas. Forest trees of sweet gum, yellow poplar, red maple, river birch, ash, and beech are brightened in spring by flowering redbud, dogwood, and shadbush. In summer abundant laurel, *magnolia virginiana,* perfumes the air with overpowering sweetness.

Aquatic life, mammals, birds, and insects abound here sheltered by its protective growth. Deer, foxes, wild turkeys, mallards, wood ducks, and, at times, Canada geese, making a stop-over on their migratory flights, are found here. Muskrats, beavers, and raccoons are abundant; mink and otter, though few in number, can also be seen along the banks. The water is filled with large-mouth bass, pike, catfish, and perch to the delight of fishermen. The northern banded river snakes, often confused with the poisonous water moccasins, are present in significant numbers, as are several species of turtles.

Most important, the Dragon is the only source of fresh water in the middle peninsula area with sufficient flow for industrial purposes or for drinking water for population centers. Either of these possibilities, if developed, would prove to be a serious threat to the ecology of this fragile environment.

The Dragon, thus, draws its uniqueness not from a single characteristic, but from the rare combination of desirable and unusual features. The stream's wildness, the rare combination of plant and animal life, and the wetland environment, now recognized as necessary to the ecology of the area, all make it remarkable.

The stream is fed by many little tributaries with such whimsical names as Briery, Timber Branch, Contrary Swamp, and Exol. Almost as large as the Dragon itself, the last gave its name to one of the oldest Baptist churches in King and Queen.

The Dragon has a slow, steady current with meandering channels and small coves. Occasionally after heavy rains, water rises to overflow its banks and create ox-bows or false turns. The waterway possesses few landmarks to serve as guides, and many intrepid hunters have been lost for hours in its swampy vastness. The fact that it has claimed several lives in recent decades may lend credence to its forbidding name.

Early settlers recongnized the value of the fertile bottom land, and many established large estates along its course. Because the flats were marshy, seventeenth and eighteenth century landowners built their homes on high ground often a mile or so away from the channel. In our vicinity, on both sides are sites of ancestral homes, a few still occupied by descendants of original owners. Among these on the Essex side are "Greenfield," "Colinbrooke," "Rose Hill" and "Montague." On the King and Queen side are "Bird Place," "Dulcie Dome," "Lewisville," "Rock Spring," "Rengardsville," "Marialva," "Laurel Bank" and "Piedmont."

Our family property, "Lewisville," was part of a 600-acre grant to Zachary Lewis in 1693. The original home, built sometime in the eighteenth century, stood at the top of Exol hill. My grandfather, William Walden, not long after he acquired the property, abandoned this site and built a smaller house on an elevation not far away just a few years before the Civil War. This house, which burned in 1968, had wide flooring and paneling in the hall--all made from Dragon cypress. My grandfather's plan was to add to it, but when the war was over, having suffered severe financial losses, he was unable to do so. The intended wing was added by my father in the 1920's.

The origin of the stream's curious name is uncertain. Perhaps the narrow, twisting channel, brown waters marked by protruding cypress knees, and its stillness under over-arching branches created an almost sinister appearance and suggested a sleeping dragon lying in wait. A different, but equally plausible theory, is that runaway slaves were lost sometimes in its watery maze; hence owners warned, "the Dragon will get you" to prevent their trying to flee. Another possibility is that some homesick Welsh settler, reminded of the small rivers of his homeland, chose the national symbol of Wales, the dragon, for the name of the stream.

In Colonial times, as today, a number of bridges crossed the Dragon. The Peter Jefferson-Joshua Frye map (1755) shows two: Bestland Bridge in Essex and Old Bridge (so designated on the map) where Route 17 crosses from Middlesex into Gloucester. The latter was established as a crossing by order of the Colonial Council in 1667. Actually the first crossing of the Dragon was a ferry, which the Council in 1664 ordered to be kept at Turk's Ferry, site of an Indian crossing in Middlesex County.

However, there were other colonial bridges. Wares Bridge, near Churchview, was in use prior to the Revolution, and Bird's Bridge, near Ino, was constructed for personal use by the Bird family, which in the 1700's owned nearly 2,000 acres of land in that vicinity. New Dragon Bridge, near Mascot, known to have been in use in the 1830's, still bears the title "new" after more than 150 years.

Also the Dragon must have been forded at many shallow places. In addition, some families maintained private bridges for personal convenience. One such was Street's Crossing used by residents of "Dulcie Dome" and "Lewisville" to reach Montague Post Office in Essex, which was less than two miles away across the stream.

The inaccessibility by land of valuable timber resources such as cypress and loblolly pine led to a survey in 1828 by Claudius Crozet of the Virginia Board of Public Works. His report stated that there was a good flow of water and that the stream could be made navigable with some improvements. He proposed that the channel be cleared of obstructions and estimated that "under cautious management it would hardly cost $1,000, a sum quite inconsiderable when compared with the benefits it would procure."

By 1839, a company had been formed to begin the work of clearing the channel from Turks' Ferry to Wares Bridge. The company was headed by Thomas W. Fauntleroy, who in 1834 had purchased a thousand-acre tract of Dragon property in Middlesex. The task consisted of removing logs, fallen trees, and submerged sandbars to make the channel navigable for bateaux and flat boats. No mechanical equipment was available then. Using only brute force, crews of men with axes, saws, picks, and shovels hacked their way through dense undergrowth to clear mile after mile. Work had to be done during periods of low water and was necessarily slow. Swarms of malaria-bearing mosquitoes attacked in the summer months. Reports to the Board of Public Works referred repeatedly to sickness holding up the work.

By 1840, about 20 miles had been cleared as far as New Dragon Bridge where a large steam saw mill was located. It had been assumed that the mill operators would use the stream to bring logs to the mill and to transport lumber to market with toll collected at certain points. However, lumber was carted overland to the Rappahannock River to be loaded on large sailing vessels for shipment to northern markets. The Dragon Swamp Navigation Company ceased operation in 1845 since little use was being made of the stretch already cleared.

Although the goal of Wares Bridge as the limit of the channel clearing effort was never reached, some landowners made an effort to keep their own stretch of the waterway cleared enough for personal use. "Lewisville" contained over 75 acres of marshland, considered worthless and carrying a very low tax value. Surrounded by marsh were two areas of high ground which locally were called islands. One of these was as large as twenty acres and was in cultivation until after the Civil War. When, in the 1920's, my father cut the timber which had reached marketable size by then, he said that corn rows were still discernible among the trees after nearly sixty years.

For my family and our neighbors long ago, the Exol and the Dragon served as a private resource as well as a playground. In summer, guests and family members went fishing for pike, perch, or catfish. Occasionally summer ducks became a temptation too strong to resist for someone, who just happened to have taken his gun along when he went fishing, and thus a duck might end on the dinner table as an unexpected feast.

In the fall the men hunted for turkeys in the forested growth at the water's edge, and boys found squirrels abundant in the oak trees. Quail nested freely in the fence rows of nearby fields, and rabbits offered chase for beagles trained to sniff out their hiding places. The raccoons which visited our cornfields in summer might be treed by coon dogs in autumn and become pelts for sale to augment a meager income. 'Possum hunting was a group activity, a frolic for boys and girls who set out with lanterns and dogs to tree the 'possum. The hunt seldom yielded game, but the walk in the crisp, night air was fun.

Muscadine vines climbed tall trees and produced thick-skinned grapes for tangy jam. Chestnut trees, now long gone because of a deadly blight, once provided nuts in abundance. Chinquapin bushes bore burrs filled with small, brown, pointed nuts which I liked to eat or to string into shiny brown necklaces to wear for an hour or two. Boys came to school with pockets bulging with nuts and

offered a handful to a favored girl. Although both chest-
nuts and chinquapins soon became wormy, gathering
them provided hours of delight.

When shingles were needed to patch a roof, my father
felled a cypress or white oak and set Uncle Combs to
splitting shingles with his frow. Sometimes in need of
extra dollars, he cut a few oak trees and hewed railroad
ties. Our firewood was secured from the woods, dead
trees as a rule, or trees blown over in a storm.

At Christmas my father and I searched for and found
luxuriant patches of running cedar and princess pine or
crow's foot, as some called it, for Christmas decorations.
We broke branches from a holly tree red with berries and
from pines because I loved the pine odor. We knew the
location of the few trees which held bunches of mistletoe
high in the branches and with great effort secured a few
pieces, careful not to take too much. Our incursions and
pleasures made no dent in nature's bounty which re-
newed itself and was undiminished for future use and
enjoyment.

The Exol stream also is the subject of many family
stories. My earliest memories are of crossing a low, very
crude bridge without a railing. I suppose the road was a
public one, but the maintenance of the bridge and the
road seemed to be a neighborhood responsibility. The
bridge was a ramshackle structure, but we blithely
trusted ourselves to it whenever we went toward Dragonville. When a prolonged rainy spell occurred, water over-
flowed into the road for yards on either side of the bridge.
Many times I've crossed when the water rose into the foot
of the buggy, and the horse appeared to be swimming for
a few feet. In winter when the water froze the crossing
was even worse; the horses, breaking through the ice,
plunged ahead, dragging the heavy vehicle, trying to get a
foothold on the ice, and breaking through at every step.

With such hazards to face, no wonder we seldom ventured abroad in winter.

When the Model-T-Ford became the mode of transportation, high water was an even greater problem because the car would "choke out" if speed produced a wave which drowned out the engine. Then, after a wait to dry off, someone had to step into knee-deep water and crank to get the engine started again. Once when we choked out coming home from a rare night outing, my father had to remove his pants and get out in the murky water, with snakes swimming from all sides toward the headlights, to crank the motor.

The benefits, however, derived from these streams far outweighed the hazards. Everyone loved and respected the Dragon and felt a proprietary responsibility toward it. We had no premonition that in the future the Dragon would face serious threats to its existence.

Now as the twentieth century draws to a close what is the future of this unique water system of marshes and streams?

It is becoming evident that this unusual stream is achieving great importance in modern Virginia. Under the Scenic Rivers Act, passed by the Virginia Assembly in 1970, the Dragon was the first Virginia waterway to receive detailed study for protection as a "wild area." A report from a study committee to the Middle Peninsula Planning Commission (1987), stated that the Smithsonian Institution had reviewed and subsequently ranked 232 ecologically significant areas throughout the Chesapeake Bay region. The Dragon system has been ranked *second.*

The Dragon's proximity to large population centers such as Fredericksburg, Richmond, and the Hampton Roads area makes it especially suitable for recreation purposes. Many urban dwellers, harassed by crowded conditions of the cities, find relief and renewal in remote areas untouched by civilization. Few such places exist in the East today. However, because of its unique character, the Dragon has remained virtually unchanged since discovery by the white man. Even today the visitor can travel by canoe for miles and not see a human habitation.

The river has long been a favorite of hunters and fishermen because of the variety of game found here. Trapping, once an important source of income from furs, is not practiced much today; but the stream offers more modern forms of recreation. Bird watching, photography and nature study draw visitors, but perhaps its greatest attraction is canoeing.

In late spring a cool greenness, a silence almost hushed in quality settles over the stream. The nearness of a striking variety of flora and fauna enchant visitors. Red-bellied sliders sun themselves on a log, water snakes glide past, woodpeckers drum on overhanging trees, trumpetvines and marsh grasses sparkle—and all so close the canoeist can reach out and break a flower as he passes. The quiet may be suddenly shattered by a cacophony of sound as a heron rookery is disturbed, but always visitors are treated to a fascinating display.

In fall the Dragon attracts campers and hunters; some hope to bag game, others to enjoy the physical challenge of the trip. Paddling may be interrupted by a submerged log or a fallen tree, for conditions are constantly changing, but passage is easy on many open stretches.

The future of this strange, beautiful, irreplaceable river is uncertain. The stream has resisted change for more than three centuries, but there are many problems involved in its protection. Dangers such as pollution, development, drainage of marsh lands, and abuse by thoughtless visitors threaten the fragile ecological structure. Those who love the Dragon for its remoteness, its wildness, and its wonderful combination of plant and animal life are eager to protect it. It is an oasis, a sanctuary in a crowded, half-mad world, that must be preserved for we cannot build another.

Canoeists on Dragon Run
(Courtesy of *The Southside Sentinel*)

Epilogue

Gradually twentieth century advances reached us. My father bought a tractor, a car, and a cream separator; my mother had an ice box and manufactured ice was delivered until she acquired an oil-burning refrigerator. The roads improved from rutted single-lane tracks to wider, smoother ones. The school children were transported by bus to a larger consolidated school. I graduated from college and became a teacher.

We lived through the Depression years and even then that necessity of modern life, electricity, had not reached our little corner of the world. Not until 1947, when REA ran a line of current from Center Cross to Dragonville did this modern marvel become available to us. By this time we had left the farm, and my father had died. The coming of electricity was one of the things to which he had looked forward eagerly. Ever the dreamer, he had anticipated the whole new way of life which it would bring to him and to his neighbors, but he did not see it.

In retrospect I marvel at how well we lived, how contented we were, and how many of the world's ills we were spared because we lived in that remote spot.

It is incredible that we who lived on the edge of the twentieth century were not an integral part of it until it was half over.

Index

To order additional copies of this book, please use coupon below.

Mail to:

(❦)

Brunswick Publishing Corporation
ROUTE 1, BOX 1-A-1
LAWRENCEVILLE, VIRGINIA 23868

Order Form

Please send me _____ copy(s) of *A Patchwork Quilt* by Louise Eubank Gray, ISBN 1-55618-061-6, LC 89-61308, at $14.95 per copy plus $3.00 mailing and handling. Virginia residents add 67¢ sales tax.

☐ Check enclosed. Charge Orders — 804-848-3865
☐ Charge to my credit card: ☐ VISA ☐ MasterCard

Card # _____ Exp. Date _____

Signature: _____

Name _____

Address _____

City _____ State _____ Zip_____

Phone # _____